UNDERWRITING
INJUSTICE

AID

and

El Salvador's

Judicial

Reform

Program

San Salvador, May 1988: Judge Serrano lies dead within his van shortly after being assassinated by unknown gunmen.

Lawyers

Committee

for

Human

Rights

UNDERWRITING INJUSTICE:

AID and

El Salvador's Judicial Reform Program

April 1989

Since 1978 the Lawyers Committee has served as a public interest law center. The Lawyers Committee works to promote international human rights law and legal procedures in the United States and abroad. The Chairman of the Lawyers Committee is Marvin Frankel; Michael Posner is its Executive Director; William G. O'Neill is the Deputy Director; Arthur Helton is Director of the Committee's Political Asylum Project.

Bound copies of this report are available from:

Lawyers Committee for Human Rights
330 Seventh Avenue
New York, NY 10001

ISBN # 0-934143-24-2

TABLE OF CONTENTS

Preface i
Introduction 1
Summary of Conclusions and Recommendations .. 12

CHAPTER I: Failed Prosecutions: 1979-1984 16

   A. Archbishop Oscar Arnulfo Romero 18
   B. Las Hojas Massacre 26
   C. Sheraton Murders 29
   D. Armenia Massacre 34

CHAPTER II: Judicial Reform Project: 1984-1989 36

   A. Commission on Investigations 41
   B. Revisory Commission on Salvadoran
      Legislation 54
   C. Judicial Protection Unit 65
   D. Judicial Administration and Training 70

CHAPTER III: Escalating Violence: 1987-1989 .. 75

   A. Recent Political Attacks 75

      San Francisco Massacre 77
      Killings at Puerta del Diablo 86
      Felix Antonio Rivera and Mario Cruz
         Rivera 90
      Los Degollados 97
      Palitos Well Case 103
      Soyapango Sand-Diggers 108
      Adrian Chavarria Giron 113
      Jose Raul Henriquez 117

   B. Attacks on the Legal and Human
      Rights Communities 120

      Judge Jorge Alberto Serrano Panameno 122
      Herbert Ernesto Anaya Sanabria 130

C. Other Targeted Sectors 147

    Humberto Centeno 149
    Manfredo Zuniga and
      Maria Ana Saenz de Zuniga 154

D. Conditions in Detention 157

    Jose Angel Alas Gomez 160
    Gerardo Hernandez Torres 162
    Manuel de Jesus Araujo Sanchez 166

CHAPTER IV: Police Training 171

These rightwing fanatics are the best friends the Soviets, the Cubans, the Sandinista comandantes, and the Salvadoran guerrillas have. Every murderous act they commit poisons the well of friendship between our two countries and advances the cause of those who would impose an alien dictatorship on the people of El Salvador. These cowardly death squad terrorists are just as repugnant to me, to President Reagan, to the U.S. Congress, and to the American people as the terrorists of the left. [....] If these death squad murders continue, you will lose the support of the American people, and that would indeed be a tragedy.

Vice President George Bush, at a dinner hosted by Provisional President Alvaro Magana in San Salvador, December 11, 1983

Death squads and terror have no place in a democracy, and I mince no words in saying it here or anywhere else. The armed forces must act with discipline in defense of the Constitution. And the judicial system must prove its capacity to cope with the terrorist acts of extremists of the right or left.

Secretary of State George P. Shultz, at a luncheon hosted by Provisional President Alvaro Magana in San Salvador, January 31, 1984

In 1983, I directly discussed the very painful issue of the 'death squads' with both President Duarte [sic] and the Salvadoran generals. In frank talks, I explained that 'death squads' were unacceptable and had to end. I explained that the United States could not, that we would not, be friends with governments that condoned the killing of political opponents. We, Salvadorans and Americans, can now be proud of the strong and swift action they took to stop that 'death squad' activity.

Statement of Vice *President* **George Bush**, *issued by the George Bush for President Campaign, 1988*

There are consequences of human rights violations in the future. We in the United States are committed to the process and system of democracy. Democracy means human rights and decency. You cannot have one without the other. Our commitment and our support [for El Salvador] is conditioned on this process and this system, and if we have violations of human rights then that is not in the spirit of the understanding that we have right now; and we will make that very, very clear.

Vice *President Dan* **Quayle**, *San Salvador, February 3, 1989*

PREFACE

This report -- the twelfth investigation by the Lawyers Committee since 1981 of human rights conditions in El Salvador -- is based on a year-long study of human rights and the administration of justice in El Salvador, including nearly four months of research in that country. It updates several earlier Committee studies -- *Justice Denied: A Report on Twelve Unresolved Human Rights Cases in El Salvador*, published in March 1985; *El Salvador: Human Rights Dismissed*, issued in July 1986; and *From the Ashes: A Report on Justice in El Salvador*, in 1987 -- and examines a number of unresolved human rights cases, renewing previous Lawyers Committee analyses of El Salvador's efforts to reform its judicial system.

The principal Lawyers Committee delegation to El Salvador visited the country from September 11 to 17, 1988. The mission was headed by John V. Lindsay, former Mayor of New York City (1966-1974) and member of the House of Representatives from New York (1959-1966). Mr. Lindsay is a partner in the New York law firm of Webster & Sheffield. He was accompanied by Scott Greathead, First Assistant Attorney General of the State of New York. Mr. Greathead, a member of the Lawyers Committee Board of Directors, has visited El Salvador 12 times on the Committee's behalf since 1982. Other members of the delegation were William P. Ford, a partner at Ford, Marrin, Esposito and Witmeyer in New York City, who has visited El Salvador as part of Lawyers Committee delegations five times, and Martha Doggett of the Lawyers Committee staff. David Fishlow of the Attorney General's Office of the State of New York provided able translation for the Messrs. Lindsay and Ford.

The delegation met with the following people in El Salvador:

Salvadoran Government and Military Officials:

Dr. Julio Alfredo Samayoa, Minister of Justice; Dr. Francisco Jose Guerrero, President of the Supreme Court; Attorney General Roberto Giron Flores; Lic. Arturo Lazo, Director of the Human Rights Department, Attorney General's office (resigned January 1989); Col. Jose Humberto Gomez, Director of the National Guard; Col Dionisio Machuca, Director of the Treasury Police; Col. Carlos Mauricio Guzman Aguilar, Director of the National Police;

i

Col. Omar Avalos and Lic. Mario Rene Castro, Vice Ministry of Public Security; Col. Juan Orlando Zepeda, Commander, First Infantry Brigade; the governmental Human Rights Commission of El Salvador (CDH); Lic. Luis Edgar Morales Joya, First Penal Judge of First Instance, San Salvador.

Members of the Human Rights Community:

Lic. Maria Julia Hernandez, Director, Tutela Legal, human rights office of the Archdiocese of San Salvador; Margaret Popkin, Assistant Director, Human Rights Institute of the Central American University, Jose Simeon Canas (IDHUCA); the nongovernmental Human Rights Commission of El Salvador (CDHES); Socorro Juridico Cristiano Arzobispo Oscar Arnulfo Romero.

The Political Community:

Col. Sigifredo Ochoa Perez, member, Legislative Assembly, ARENA; Dr. Guillermo Ungo, presidential candidate, Democratic Convergence; Dr. Mario Reni Roldan, Social Democratic Party, Vice-Presidential Candidate, Democratic Convergence.

U.S. Embassy officials:

Ambassador William Graham Walker; David Dloughy, Deputy Chief of Mission; Hank Bassford, Chief of Mission, Agency for International Development; Stephen McFarland, Chief Political Officer; Gail Lecce and Roberto Figueredo, Office of Democratic Initiatives, Agency for International Development; Peter B. Schmeelk, Human Rights Officer.

Ms. Doggett conducted additional research in El Salvador from May 16-31, 1988; June 28-July 16, 1988; September 7-October 6, 1988; and January 2-20, 1989. Jemera Rone, El Salvador representative for the Lawyers Committee, has provided ongoing monitoring of the situation there since 1985. Her thorough research and insightful analysis have proved invaluable in the Committee's work. Many of the cases in this report are based on Ms. Rone's fact-finding.

Lawyers Committee staff conducted the following additional interviews in El Salvador:

U.S. Embassy officials:

David S. Kitson, Office of Democratic Initiatives, AID; Ray Gagnon, U.S. Consultant, Special Investigative Unit; Major Alfonso Gomez; Janice Ellmore, Political Officer.

Members of the Judiciary and Legal Community:

Attorney General Roberto Alvarado Garcia (named January 1989); Sotero Consuett Diaz, Human Rights Department, Attorney General's office; Dr. Juan Hector Larios Larios, Third Penal Judge, San Salvador; Dr. Consuelo Salazar de Revelo, First Penal Judge, Zacatecoluca; Carlos Roberto Urbina, First Instance Judge, Tonacatepeque; Dr. Simon Kafie Olmedo, Third Military Judge of First Instance; Dr. Ricardo A. Zamora, Fourth Penal Judge of First Instance, San Salvador; Dr. Dora del Carmen Gomez de Claros, First Instance Judge, Dulce Nombre de Maria; Dr. Jorge Alberto Carcamo Quintana, Secretary General, Commission on Investigations; Dr. Jose Ernesto Criollo, Executive Secretary, Revisory Commission on Salvadoran Legislation (CORELESAL).

Members of the Political Community:

Lic. Ruben Zamora, General Coordinator, Democratic Convergence; President-elect Alfredo Cristiani, ARENA; Fidel Chavez Mena, presidential candidate, Christian Democratic Party (PDC).

Other individuals and groups:

Col. Rene Emilio Ponce, Chief of Staff of the Armed Forces; the International Committee of the Red Cross; Danilo Umana Sacasa, Director of Human Rights, National Union of Workers and Peasants (UNOC); Humberto Centeno, National Unity of

iii

Salvadoran Workers (UNTS); Lic. Matias Romero Coto, governmental Human Rights Commission of El Salvador.

Additional interviews were conducted by the Lawyers Committee staff in Washington, D.C. with officials who oversee El Salvador policy at the Agency for International Development and the Department of State and with government officials in charge of police training under the Anti-Terrorism Assistance program and the International Criminal Investigative Training Assistance Program (ICITAP).

We would like to express special thanks to Margaret Popkin of the Central American University in San Salvador, who generously opened her files and provided useful critique to drafts; to Kathy DeRiemer; and to Maryam Elahi, an attorney working at the Lawyers Committee through the International Human Rights Internship Program. We are also grateful to Robert Weiner, a consultant to Americas Watch, who generously shared his research throughout the project and wrote the chapters on Archbishop Romero and the San Francisco massacre.

Finally, we wish to thank members of the Salvadoran human rights community, without whose guidance and input this report would not have been possible. A number of the victims, family members, judges, attorneys, and human rights activists we interviewed asked that their names not be used because they fear for their own safety.

The report was written by Martha Doggett of the Committee's Human Rights Program on Latin America and the Caribbean and edited by William O'Neill and Michael Posner.

New York, New York
April 1989

INTRODUCTION

On March 19, Alfredo Cristiani of the rightist Nationalist Republican Alliance (ARENA) emerged victorious from El Salvador's bitter presidential contest, and will assume office on June 1. For almost a decade, the country which Cristiani will attempt to govern has been locked in the painful turbulence of civil war. Now, political violence -- including killings and state-sponsored disappearances -- is once again on the rise, after declining between 1983 and 1987. For the last 18 months, these and other serious abuses have been increasing at an alarming rate, with no indication that they are being brought under control. The violence, coupled with steadily deteriorating social and economic conditions, has forced several hundred thousand Salvadorans to flee the country, while several hundred thousand more have been displaced internally by the fighting.

Few families are untouched by the violence; a generation of children is growing up knowing only war. Recently, one besieged judge expressed his fear that future violence would surpass the levels of the early 1980's. Incredulous, we asked a top official in the Attorney General's office whether he agreed. "We won't relive the 1980's," he told us, "because every stage has its own logic. But the violence could get worse than it was then because now so many more are armed." Stemming the violence while addressing its root causes is the ominous challenge facing the country's new president.

The San Francisco Massacre: A Return to the Past?

While it is difficult to predict the future, a number of disturbing trends signal a deepening human rights crisis. The San Francisco massacre is indicative of this crisis. Last September, troops from the Fifth Brigade detained 10 peasants whose names appeared on the soldiers' list. The next morning relatives found their bodies in a gully near their homes in San Francisco, Department of San Vicente. Most had died from a shot to the head; the presence of powder burns indicated they had been shot at close range.

The incident is the largest reported mass killing by the military since the 1984 massacre of 34 peasants at Las Vueltas. It is the kind of wanton killing of non-combatants that officials in San Salvador and Washington have insisted could no longer occur.

Emboldened by Salvadoran government promises to investigate human rights crimes, family members vigorously pursued

1

the San Francisco case, prompting the Attorney General's office to obtain an exhumation order in hopes of legally establishing the cause of death. As the bodies were lifted from the ground, military helicopters swooped in over the grave site while soldiers hovered on the edge of the crowd of onlookers. "See the conditions we have to work under," an official from the Attorney General's office told a Lawyers Committee representative indignantly. "This too is a form of harassment."

While some court authorities have made good faith attempts to pursue the case, others have stalled or thrown up obstacles.[1] The major barrier, however, has been the military itself. Despite some 30 eyewitness depositions and forensic evidence that the 10 had been shot execution-style, the military refused to provide complete information on those soldiers who were involved, and maintained its version of events -- that the 10 had died in a guerrilla ambush.

Frustrated at the lack of progress in this and other cases in which the evidence of the Armed Forces' guilt was overwhelming, the Bush Administration sent Vice President Dan Quayle to El Salvador in early February to press the issue of human rights with the Salvadoran military High Command.[2] Following his meetings, the Government of El Salvador issued yet another promise to investigate the September massacre. Within weeks, however, it became clear that there was little likelihood this promise would be fulfilled. *The Washington Post* of February 25, 1989 reported that the Vice President's "demands infuriated the Army. Military sources said no investigation of the [San Francisco] killings is underway despite public assurances to the contrary."[3]

Writing about the same case in early February, James LeMoyne of *The New York Times* predicted the Army's stance:

> American officials claim to be demanding "action" on the case -- a perennial, now almost laughable, promise that they have never had the courage to act

---

[1]See p.77 for a discussion of the San Francisco massacre.

[2]El Salvador's Armed Forces include the military and the Security Forces. The Security Forces, the country's police corps, consist of the National Guard, the Treasury Police, and the National Police.

[3]*The Washington Post*, February 25, 1989.

2

upon when army officers decide, as they have in this case, to tell the American Embassy to go to hell.[4]

But U.S. officials continued to "demand action," and the Ministry of Defense has now disavowed its own version of events, asserting that officers in charge of the operation had misled their commanders. A Ministry communique issued March 13 said a major, a sublieutenant, three lower ranking officers, and four enlisted men would be tried in a civilian court for their roles in the massacre. While we welcome these recent developments, past practice gives us little reason to be hopeful that those responsible will be held accountable before the law.

A Judicial System Close to Paralysis

The government's near paralysis in the San Francisco killings is merely the latest in a long line of its failures to hold members of the Armed Forces accountable for political violence. In thousands of these cases, dating back to the 1980 assassination of Archbishop Oscar Arnulfo Romero, the Salvadoran military has refused to assist prosecutions. In fact, in many cases senior military officials have blatantly interfered with investigations or prosecutions, preventing them from being carried out.

Lack of cooperation by the Armed Forces effectively prevents virtually all human rights cases from being resolved. Under Salvadoran law, evidence introduced in court must be produced either by an investigating judge or an auxiliary organ of the judiciary. This provision creates paralysis: the only auxiliary organs with authority to bring evidence in cases involving the Security Forces are the Security Forces themselves.

The military's debilitating role in these cases, coupled with the civilian government's inability or unwillingness to make fundamental changes, has brought El Salvador's judicial system dangerously close to collapse. Today, that system is wracked by fear, intimidation, and political meddling. Judges and lawyers are regularly subjected to bribery attempts and threats of violence. Several courageous judges and lawyers who sought to advance justice in sensitive cases have resigned in the past year, fearful of the consequences of pursuing the truth.

---

[4]*The New York Times Magazine*, February 5, 1989.

"Nobody respects the law," one judge told the Committee. "Everybody tries to make their own justice. If they don't agree with the judge's decision, they just kill him." In May 1988, Dr. Jorge Alberto Serrano, became the third judge to meet that fate in as many years. Judge Serrano was killed while presiding over a politically explosive case involving a kidnapping-for-profit ring run by rightist forces. Dr. Serrano died just days before he was expected to rule on an amnesty petition filed by defense attorneys for three men held since 1986 in connection with the case, two of them former military officers. It was widely reported that Judge Serrano was under considerable pressure to grant amnesty to the men, and had rejected a number of bribery attempts. He had also been the presiding judge in the 1985 Zona Rosa case in which nine civilians and four U.S. marines were killed.

A sweeping amnesty law promulgated in October 1987 has only further discouraged those judges and attorneys who are honestly seeking justice. Understandably, many are now unwilling to risk harassment, and perhaps even death, because they believe even the most brutal criminal acts are likely to be forgiven no matter what they do.

Intimidation of the Judiciary

"We are living in a drama," one courageous judge told the Lawyers Committee. "Justice in many areas is a masquerade, and sometimes they don't even allow us to be good actors."

Relating the conclusions that emerged from a symposium for judges convened by the Supreme Court, one judge outlined conditions now imposed on the judiciary:

> In cases involving regular people, you can apply the law as needed. In cases involving lower ranking soldiers acting on their own, you are subjected to certain pressures, but not serious problems. In cases involving high-ranking officers or low-ranking officers acting on orders of a higher authority, practically speaking you can't do anything.[5]

Intimidation and harassment can take many forms: a caller who says, "We know where your son is"; the military attorney who

---

[5]Lawyers Committee interview, San Salvador, September 1988.

regularly visits the courthouse, pressuring witnesses; an exhumation hindered by soldiers who refuse to let the judicial party pass a roadblock because "we can't guarantee your safety."

One judge who has received death threats is Dr. Consuelo Salazar de Revelo, First Penal Judge of Zacatecoluca. In January 1988, Dr. Salazar de Revelo denied amnesty to five National Guardsmen who were convicted in 1984 for the 1980 rape and murder of four U.S. churchwomen. After the ruling, she began receiving death threats, she told the Lawyers Committee, and was provided with bodyguards for two months by the U.S. Embassy. A Special Investigative Unit formed in 1985 to handle human rights cases lists these threats among its active investigations. On June 27, 1988, the five guardsmen appealed again for amnesty, which was again denied. "As the whole world knows," they wrote in their request, "the assassinated nuns belonged to a leftist religious order which participated in terrorist plans...."[6]

Another judge presiding over an early, unresolved human rights case has also been threatened. Dora del Carmen Gomez de Claros, the judge in northern Dulce Nombre de Maria, began receiving weekly threatening phone calls after she reopened the case of four Dutch journalists murdered in 1981. One caller even told her he was calling from the Headquarters of the Fourth Brigade. The four-hour journey from San Salvador, where her family lives, became risky. Buses travelling north to Chalatenango, a conflictive zone,[7] are regularly searched at a military checkpoint. Several times she has been pulled off to the side by soldiers who say, "you're the judge." Judge Gomez de Claros told the *San Francisco Examiner*, "It wasn't worth it becoming a judge. Maybe at a different time in history, but not now. For me, the justice system here doesn't

---

[6]The Lawyers Committee reviewed court documents in the case at the Zacatecoluca court house on October 1, 1988.

[7]In El Salvador, the term "conflictive zone" indicates an area of the country in which guerrillas are active, where combat is apt to occur, and which may be in FMLN hands one day, and under Army dominance the next.

5

work."[8] The Judge and her family have recently been accepted into a Canadian immigration program.

Another judge assigned to a post near a conflictive zone who travels to work from his home in San Salvador told of his fear of investigating a case in an area where the FMLN is active. "If the guerrillas didn't get me, the military would assume I was one of them," he told the Lawyers Committee.

Resignations of Justices of the Peace

In a disturbing recent trend, members of the judiciary appear now to be facing serious threats from the left as well as from the military. In late 1988, the Farabundo Marti National Liberation Front (FMLN) stepped up its campaign to undercut the presence and authority of the government at the local level, predicated on the assumption that many of these local officials form integral links in counterinsurgency efforts. First, numerous mayors were told to leave their posts within 72 hours, or face execution. Eight have been killed in the last year; over 100 have heeded the warning and turned in their resignations.

Early this year, these threats extended to Justices of the Peace, who carry out the most basic judicial tasks at the local level. According to accounts in the Salvadoran press, at least seven justices resigned under FMLN pressure. *Jueces de paz* in Tapalhuaca, La Paz; San Ildefonso, San Vicente; Ereguayquin and Nueva Granada, both in Usulutan; Metapan, Santa Ana; Villa Dolores, Cabanas; and Oratorio de Concepcion, Cuzcatlan have all submitted resignations to the Supreme Court, according to press reports.[9]

According to Tutela Legal, the human rights office of the Archdiocese of San Salvador, the Justice of the Peace of Carolina, San Miguel, was killed on June 14, 1988 by the FMLN. Jose Apolinario Martinez had received a letter on May 2, 1987, warning him to resign "or he would pay the consequences." The Lawyers Committee is greatly concerned by these recent developments, which

---

[8]Judge Gomez de Claros was interviewed by the Lawyers Committee on September 23, 1988 and by a Lawyers Committee associate on December 1, 1988. See also *San Francisco Examiner*, December 11, 1988.

[9]*La Prensa Grafica*, January 14, 1989; *Diario de Hoy*, January 13 and 14, 1989.

6

are today contributing to the breakdown of the rule of law in El Salvador.

Efforts to Revitalize the Judicial System

In 1984, the government of El Salvador initiated efforts to restore the country's enfeebled judicial system. Drawing on funds from the U.S. Agency for International Development (AID), the government embarked on a program designed to revise outmoded laws, train judges and court personnel, investigate politically sensitive crimes, and protect judges, jurors, and others who are involved in such cases.

The AID-funded project was divided into four parts, a Commission on Investigations and under it a Special Investigative Unit, a Judicial Protection Unit, a Legal Revisory Commission and a Judicial Training Program. Initiated to "build and sustain confidence" in the Salvadoran judicial system, after more than four years the program has failed dramatically. In 1987 the Lawyers Committee concluded that "without the political will to ensure the fundamental integrity of the justice system of El Salvador, no amount of technical aid, training, revision of the laws, or special units will inspire confidence in that system."[10] Regrettably, over two years later, El Salvador's human rights situation has deteriorated significantly and little has been accomplished to restore an independent judicial system that might be capable of ameliorating the current human rights crisis.

The Special Investigative Unit (SIU), staffed by military detectives and said to work under the direction of civilians in the Commission on Investigations, was mandated to tackle the most sensitive human rights cases. In practice, there is little evidence that the SIU is under civilian control. Its detectives have foregone investigations of excesses by their military colleagues, focussing instead on common crimes and corruption cases. For all the SIU's efforts -- and $3.5 million in U.S. support[11] -- there is no noticeable

---

[10]*From the Ashes: A Report on Justice in El Salvador* (Lawyers Committee for Human Rights, 1987), p.5.

[11]The Commission's budget totals $5.5 million. The additional $2 million is Salvadoran counterpart funds, which are actually local currency generated from Economic Support Funds received from the United States. As such, it is fair to say that the entire program budget comes from the United States.

difference in the capacity of the Salvadoran judicial system to investigate and prosecute serious violations by the Armed Forces, the kinds of cases which the SIU was meant to pursue. "Military officers or members of the Security Forces are sacred cows," a judge told us.

The Revisory Commission, designed to evaluate the judicial system and the existing body of laws and draft appropriate reform legislation, has produced only meager results after three and a half years. Only one draft law has been passed by the Legislative Assembly. Much of the Commission's activity has focussed on theoretical studies of the judicial system. While potentially useful, few have immediate practical application that could improve the country's dire human rights situation.

A Judicial Protection Unit, designed to protect participants in sensitive cases, was used in only a few instances and was then disbanded. Allocated funds have remained in escrow for years, pending the outcome of seemingly endless discussions among U.S. and Salvadoran policymakers. The reform program's fourth component, the training of judges and judicial personnel, as well as other technical support to the court system, can at best improve the system's efficiency. Given the near collapse of the judicial system, this aid remains insignificant.

While these programs, along with related initiatives, have helped to make the language of human rights the idiom of the day in El Salvador, they have failed to change the operating practices of the Salvadoran military. Not only have attempts to launch investigations of new violations been thwarted in recent months, but there has been a continued failure to resolve much publicized older cases that initially catalyzed the reform programs. Among these are the 1983 massacre of Indian peasants at Las Hojas and the 1980 murder of Archbishop Romero.

Archbishop Romero

Roman Catholic Archbishop Oscar Romero was shot as he said mass at the Divine Providence Hospital on March 24, 1980. He was an outspoken critic of the government's and military's human rights record. Just weeks before his death, Archbishop Romero wrote to President Carter, pleading with him to stop supporting El Salvador's Armed Forces. Roberto D'Aubuisson, founder of the right-wing ARENA party, and several of his close associates have been implicated in the murder, yet today, almost nine years later, the case is further from resolution than ever.

8

Through the years the case has been a point of contention between the Christian Democratic and ARENA parties in their own struggle for power. Last December, the Supreme Court -- dominated by ARENA appointees -- threw out an extradition request for a D'Aubuisson protege who had sought refuge in Miami, effectively stalling any hopes for progress.

Four days later, Salvadoran Attorney General Roberto Giron Flores, appointed by the Christian Democractic Assembly in June 1987, was ousted. Meeting on December 23, 1988, the ARENA-dominated Legislative Assembly removed the Attorney General from his post, citing incompetence and misconduct, including improper filing of the extradition request. Hinting at what was to follow, ARENA deputy Roberto D'Aubuisson, who acted as floor manager for the vote, told a San Salvador morning daily that "the plenary at two in the afternoon this Friday will be historic."[12]

Giron Flores told a U.S. reporter: "The truth is that I was fired for a simple and fundamental reason -- because the Romero case was about to be resolved. The Romero case is now closed, and I was fired so the case could be closed."[13] Giron Flores has challenged his ouster before the Supreme Court, arguing that the Assembly can only remove an Attorney General for mental or physical incapacity or for having committed a crime. The ARENA-dominated Assembly has now appointed Dr. Roberto Garcia Alvarado -- a lawyer with no demonstrated commitment to pursuing human rights cases -- to this critical post.

Role of the United States

The United States government continues to play a central role in virtually all aspects of Salvadoran life. Since 1980 the United States has provided more than $3 billion in military and economic aid to El Salvador. Despite its pervasive presence and involvement, many U.S. policymakers seem unwilling to acknowledge the dimensions of the current human rights crisis. A State Department report in December, for example, notes casually, and without further analysis:

> The Salvadoran government appears fully committed to eliminating [political] violence [...] While abuses

---

[12]*La Prensa Grafica*, December 23, 1988.

[13]*The Washington Post*, December 29, 1988.

9

continue to occur, they do not appear to be carried out on orders from above, but rather are the isolated, unsanctioned actions of soldiers acting on their own.[14]

Such misleading statements do little to advance the cause of human rights. Nor does the continued advocacy of initiatives such as the Administration of Justice Programs, absent serious reconsideration of how such programs are being carried out and what they are achieving.

An Evaluation of the Administration of Justice Program

We find ourselves in agreement with the judge who, when asked his opinion of the AID-funded reform program, told the Lawyers Committee: "I don't know who the money is helping, because there is no more justice in El Salvador." Another San Salvador criminal judge complained that the program offered "U.S. solutions to Salvadoran problems."

We also question the wisdom of creating new institutions which parallel the country's existing justice system. Rather than addressing problems and weaknesses in current structures, AID has fostered the creation of new ones: a Special Investigative Unit to facilitate the investigation of military violations; a Judicial Protection Unit to provide security in a country where little security can be ensured; model courts to show how a court should really function.[15]

In our view, these parallel institutions have reproduced many existing problems while adding new ones. Under the Commission on Investigations, police detectives have proved no more capable of independently and objectively investigating military violators than they were when working directly under the Security Forces. And now, with an additional institution playing a role in the judicial process, other branches of the system complain of lack of information and of having their hands tied while they await an SIU briefing. Further, in several cases everybody seemed to be waiting for the other group to start an investigation. While the Commission on Investigations is clearly mandated to launch an inquiry, Justice

---

[14]"Report on the Situation in El Salvador," Department of State, December 1, 1988.

[15]Five "model courts" were to be established by the third quarter of FY 1988; they are now slated for mid 1989. For a discussion of these model courts, see p.73.

10

Minister Samayoa defended the Commission's failure to order the SIU to look into a notorious human rights case because "no one asked them to."

One frustrated Salvadoran human rights worker, characterized the Judicial Reform efforts in the following terms:

> What they have done is strengthen *injustice*. The military, which should be conducting investigations, is actually interfering with judicial power. For the first time, an institution has been created that unifies civilians and the military to violate human rights. Before they were separate; now we have one civilian-military body, and the civilians have been compromised. The Minister of Justice has become a mouthpiece for military men.[16]

Police Training

A 1974 amendment to the U.S. Foreign Assistance Act banned the use of foreign aid monies for police training. Despite this prohibition, U.S. training of El Salvador's Security Forces has increased along with other forms of U.S. involvement through a variety of other training options and loopholes. Today, Salvadoran police are being educated and supplied through at least seven different U.S. programs.

U.S. officials in Washington and San Salvador express satisfaction with the results of this training, pointing to greater professionalism and better police performance in the context of crowd control. While there has been improvement from the days when El Salvador's Security Forces gunned down mourners at Archbishop Romero's funeral, the Lawyers Committee does not find further U.S. training warranted. Credible reports of physical and psychological torture and mistreatment in detention centers and prisons persist. U.S. training has apparently been ineffective in stopping these practices.

---

[16]Lawyers Committee interview, San Salvador, January 1989.

11

SUMMARY OF CONCLUSIONS:

Based on examination of El Salvador's judicial system, and the current human rights situation in that country, the Lawyers Committee offers the following conclusions and recommendations:

1. There has been a disturbing increase in the number of political killings, including death squad-style executions, in El Salvador in the last year. The pattern of these gross violations suggests that officers of the Salvadoran Armed and Security Forces are either directly involved or unwilling to take appropriate measures to prevent future abuses from occurring.

2. Though the number of political prisoners and administrative detainees has declined appreciably in the last few years, those who are detained are often subjected to physical and psychological abuse. In recent months the Lawyers Committee has continued to receive reports of beatings, sleep deprivation, denials of food and water, and threats of grave physical danger to detainees and their families. Many of these abusive practices occur in the first few days of detention, as members of the Salvadoran Security Forces seek to obtain information about FMLN activities.

3. A review of the investigations into recent human rights cases and prior violations reveals a record of almost complete failure. Officers of the military and El Salvador's three Security Forces are practically immune from successful prosecution, even in cases where ample evidence exists to bring them to trial. In most cases the military has refused to cooperate in investigations into these crimes, and often military officers have obstructed such investigations. The problems resulting from the government's reluctance to investigate longstanding cases, such as the Las Hojas massacre and the killing of two U.S. labor advisors and their Salvadoran colleague, were exacerbated by a sweeping amnesty law enacted in October 1987. Even in the few cases that were outside the scope of the amnesty, there has been no progress in holding officers accountable.

4. Among those who have been targetted for political assassination, intimidation, or other forms of mistreatment are judges, lawyers, human rights activists, Church members and leaders, opposition political figures, and labor activists.

5. The Administration of Justice Program, a U.S.-funded project initiated to encourage the prosecution of human rights cases, has failed to address these problems. The program aims to address problems caused in part by outmoded laws, ill-trained judges and

investigators, and a lack of material support and equipment. Thus far the program has made little progress toward enabling the government of El Salvador to hold members of the Armed Forces accountable for acts of political violence.

Recommendations to the Government of El Salvador:

1. Through the Revisory Commission or other appropriate bodies, steps should be taken to amend the laws and Constitution to designate the Special Investigative Unit, the Attorney General's Office, and other relevant civilian agencies as auxiliary organs of the judiciary. This step would facilitate impartial investigations of Armed Forces personnel accused of committing human rights crimes.

2. The Attorney General's Office, the Special Investigative Unit, and other appropriate bodies should take prompt and decisive steps to renew the government's commitment to prosecute those responsible for the 1980 assassination of Archbishop Romero. Investigations and prosecutions of recent cases should also be undertaken, including the 1988 San Francisco massacre, and the *Puerta del Diablo* killings.

3. The Attorney General's Office or the SIU should also commence thorough investigations of all reports of torture by Security Forces. In cases where credible evidence is present, Security Force members should be suspended until these investigations are completed.

4. Strict compliance with the 72-hour limit on administrative detention should be demanded and enforced. To demonstrate its compliance with international human rights standards, the government should permit immediate access to new detainees by delegates of the International Committee of the Red Cross.

5. The Armed Forces of El Salvador should undergo a major restructuring. The objective of this restructuring should be to remove the three Security Forces -- the National Police, Treasury Police and National Guard -- from the command of the Salvadoran military, placing them under appropriate civilian authority. Further, the government should take steps to ensure that the Armed Forces cooperate fully with government agencies in investigations of human rights violations committed by military personnel.

6. A thorough and public investigation should be made of death squad activities within the military and Security Forces. All members of the Armed Forces who are found to have any current

or past involvement in death squad activities should be publicly identified and immediately removed from government service.

Recommendations To the Government of the United States:

1. A comprehensive evaluation of the Administration of Justice Program (AOJ) should be undertaken. Until this review is completed, further U.S. participation and funding for this program should be suspended, including those funds already allocated but not expended.

2. With respect to the Commission on Investigations, the U.S. government should evaluate the time and resources the Commission and its Special Investigative Unit (SIU) have devoted to human rights cases as compared to other types of crimes. The result of this evaluation should be made public.

3. In this evaluation, the U.S. government should also seek to determine by what criteria SIU cases are chosen, and how resources are allocated.

4. The AOJ evaluation should also focus on recent cases of harassment, intimidation and physical violence against judges, lawyers and others involved in the judicial process. It should explore options for protecting these people in the future.

5. The U.S. Congress should closely monitor current Executive Branch reports on human rights conditions, and should urge the State Department and other Executive Branch Agencies to submit revised reports when initial submissions are incomplete or misleading.

6. The Lawyers Committee also urges Congress to review existing anti-terrorism and other programs that circumvent Section 660 of the Foreign Assistance Act. Congress should take steps to stop current and additional funding for the Salvadoran police, including training under the Administration of Justice Program, and to enact legislation closing existing loopholes. Specifically, we recommend that Congress should: a) pass legislation barring the use of Anti-Terrorism Assistance funds for the training of police forces to combat domestic insurgency and b) bar the use of military Assistance Program funds for police training, regardless of whether the police are performing military or quasi-military duties.

The San Francisco massacre, September 21, 1988.
(photo: Corinne Dufka)

7. Over the years, several U.S. government bodies have investigated death squad activity in El Salvador. The findings of these inquiries should be made public. A thorough study of recent activity should be conducted, and a list of names of members of the military and Security Forces who have been or are implicated in death squad killings should be released. Until death squad killers are given names and faces, these paramilitary forces will remain a convenient excuse for continued political violence in El Salvador.

CHAPTER I: FAILED PROSECUTIONS (1979-1984)

For nearly a decade, El Salvador has been engaged in a bitter civil war. In the course of the fighting, tens of thousands of civilian non-combatants have been killed. Credible reports by human rights organizations in El Salvador and abroad have linked many of these political killings to the Salvadoran Armed Forces and death squads that are either drawn from or have close links to the military.

In the early 1980's, there were an average of more than 800 political murders a month, a staggering number for a country of some five million people. Among the early victims of this political violence was the Archbishop of San Salvador, Oscar Arnulfo Romero. The government's failure to properly investigate this case and several other widely publicized cases from this period drew worldwide attention to El Salvador's reign of terror, and led ultimately to some initiatives designed to improve the country's human rights record, including a series of measures to revitalize El Salvador's judicial system.

An Examination of Key Early Cases

In 1985 the Lawyers Committee published *Justice Denied*, a report examining investigative efforts in the Romero case and eleven other human rights cases. In 1986 and again in 1987, the Committee updated the status of the investigations in these cases. In our 1987 report the Committee noted that while the campaign of political murder has become less ambitious than it was in the early 1980's, it has never been conclusively repudiated nor its perpetrators punished. The report concluded: "Until [these killers] are prosecuted and convicted, political murder will always remain an option in El Salvador's public life, and the Salvadoran justice system will always be suspect."[17]

Each of the four cases described below was identified by President Duarte in 1984 as a priority case for his new administration. Following his inauguration in the spring of 1984, he created a special commission to investigate these cases, noting the symbolic significance of bringing the perpetrators of these crimes to justice. Each of these cases has received widespread publicity and attention, both in El Salvador and abroad. Each of these cases -- now seven, eight, and nine years old -- provides a dramatic

---

[17]*From the Ashes*, p.13.

17

illustration of the lengths to which the Salvadoran Armed Forces have gone to protect their own against civilian control or accountability.

A. MURDER OF ARCHBISHOP OSCAR ARNULFO ROMERO
March 24, 1980

The Murder

Monsignor Oscar Arnulfo Romero, Archbishop of San Salvador, was shot in the chest as he said mass on March 24, 1980 in a chapel at the Divine Providence cancer hospital. Three days after his death, the judge assigned to the case narrowly escaped an assassination attempt by two men who shot and wounded his housekeeper.[18] The judge fled the country.

Because of Romero's position in the Church and his efforts to promote respect for human rights, the pursuit of his killers has remained a significant indicator of El Salvador's progress toward establishing civilian authority and the rule of law. The case is the only political murder that was specifically exempted from the sweeping October 1987 amnesty.

The Investigation

Shortly after the killings, the National Police launched an investigation of the case, only to abandon it six weeks later. Few appeared willing to openly discuss the murder with police agents; memoranda from the investigation's lead detective[19] show that no useful information was gathered at the chapel, at the hospital where the Archbishop was rushed after the shooting or at the offices of opposition newspaper publisher Jorge Pinto.[20]

The unit suspended its investigation in May 1980. According to court files, detectives had accomplished little more than to

---

[18]See *El Salvador: Human Rights Dismissed, A Report on 16 Unresolved Cases*, (Lawyers Committee for Human Rights, 1986) pp. 29-34.

[19]A Lawyers Committee representative reviewed the court files in 1987 and 1988. The information on the investigation by the National Police was gleaned from police documents in these court files.

[20]At the time of the shooting, Archbishop Romero was saying an anniversary mass in commemoration of the death of Pinto's mother. Most of those in attendance were Pinto's family, friends, and employees.

determine that the fatal shot probably came through the chapel's open front doors and that a vehicle might have been used. These detectives' reports include no information on the calibre of the fatal bullet or the type of weapon used, and statements from only four of the more than two dozen witnesses at the scene. The search yielded no suspects.

The detectives' best clue -- license plates on the getaway car used in the aborted attempt on the judge's life -- lay fallow until long after the investigation had been discontinued. The judge himself, who from exile accused former National Guard Major Roberto D'Aubuisson and former National Guard Colonel Jose Medrano of hiring Romero's killers, would not have been surprised: he testified that police agents were stationed some 200 meters from his house throughout the attack.[21]

The Attorney General's office subsequently investigated the case, with seemingly little more success. Jose Francisco Guerrero, a member of Roberto D'Aubuisson's right-wing ARENA party and once his personal attorney, was named Attorney General in mid-1984. Within months, having concluded that his investigators had no leads, Guerrero discontinued the investigation. A separate Investigative Commission of the President, mandated in 1984 by

---

[21]*Report on Human Rights in El Salvador* (Americas Watch/American Civil Liberties Union, 1982), pp. 102-103.
Despite the former judge's published statements connecting the Romero case with the attack on his life, the judge currently assigned to both cases continues to insist that the two incidents are factually and legally unrelated. (Lawyers Committee interview with Dr. Ricardo Zamora, Fourth Penal Judge, San Salvador, January 12, 1989.)
While D'Aubuisson left his post in military intelligence following the October 1979 young officers coup, he reportedly continued on the Armed Forces payroll. See *New York Times*, March 3, 1984. D'Aubuisson is generally referred to as a "cashiered officer," yet one account said the major "asked to be discharged because, he said, he couldn't go along with the left-leanings of the new government." See Christopher Dickey, "Behind the Death Squads," *The New Republic*, December 26, 1983.

newly elected President Duarte to investigate the Romero and four other human rights cases, achieved very little.[22]

A False Witness

The Romero case returned to national attention briefly in 1985 with the appearance of Adalberto Salazar Collier, an ex-convict who turned himself over to the National Guard in May 1985 asking for protection. Salazar claimed to have been coerced into "confessing" to a role in the Romero assassination on a videotape produced by right-wing businessmen and Salvadoran, Honduran, and Venezuelan military officers.[23]

Imprisoned in late 1981 in Tegucigalpa on trumped-up charges by Honduran secret police, Salazar said, he was pressured by military officials to inform on political prisoners in detention with him.

After several months, Salazar said, he was visited by a Salvadoran Army colonel, Ricardo Pena Arbaiza.[24] According to Salazar, Col. Pena Arbaiza soon began training him to impersonate a guerrilla commander, and ultimately helped obtain his release from prison. Soon after, with the help of Venezuelan Col. Ivan

---

[22]See *From the Ashes: A Report on Justice in El Salvador*, (Lawyers Committee for Human Rights, 1987), p.14. The "Cestoni Commission," as President's Duarte's investigative body was known, apparently only seriously investigated one of the five cases in its portfolio, the Armenia well killings.

[23]This account is based on court documents reviewed by a Lawyers Committee representative. Salazar Collier made a declaration to the judge of San Salvador's Fourth Penal Court on August 23, 1985; his statement to the National Guard was recorded in November 1985.

[24]Shortly before Salvadoran soldiers murdered four U.S. churchwomen in December 1980, Col. Arbaiza, then a commanding officer in Chalatenango, threatened Ita Ford and Maura Clarke, who were working in that department. Ita Ford told her family that Arbaiza had called the sisters "subversives" because they were working with the poor. See also Robert Armstrong and Janet Shenk, *El Salvador: The Face of Revolution* (South End Press, 1982), p. 175.

21

Gonzalez, an interview was arranged with two journalists in which Salazar was instructed to identify himself as ex-FMLN "Commander Lobo," and to admit to a role in the Romero murder.[25] Later, Salazar said, he was pressured into repeating the fiction on videotape. Within days of making the tape, he fled his home in northern Honduras when unidentified men came looking for him.

Only after returning to El Salvador did Salazar discover that his video had been presented on Salvadoran television by Roberto D'Aubuisson. Salazar then decided to seek protection.

Court records in the Romero case indicate that Salazar was imprisoned in El Salvador throughout the time surrounding the Romero murder, and therefore he could not have taken part in the killing. Roberto D'Aubuisson denied knowledge of the tape's illicit origins, telling reporters that it had been given to the ARENA party by unknown persons. Col. Pena Arbaiza admitted only to knowing Salazar from his visits to the Tegucigalpa penitentiary on behalf of Christian Fellowship Ministries, and to having tried unsuccessfully to use him as an informant.

Although attracting headlines, these developments had little impact on the investigation, which was suspended by May 1986 by Attorney General Guerrero, an ARENA founder. Ousted by the Christian Democrat-controlled legislature, Guerrero had recently been reinstated to his post by the Supreme Court.

A New Witness

In November 1987, President Duarte made a dramatic claim that he had solved the case. His announcement[26] was based on the testimony of Antonio Amado Garay, who said he had chauffeured

---

[25]According to Salazar's testimony to the National Guard, he was interviewed in early 1984 by a Costa Rican journalist named Orlando Gastro and an unnamed Venezuelan journalist.

[26]Duarte's televised press conference was held in the heat of the campaign leading up to elections in March 1988 and was widely considered to be politically motivated. After years in exile, opposition leaders Guillermo Ungo and Ruben Zamora made triumphant homecomings that same month, and the rival right-wing ARENA party was expected to do well in the March polling. Observers in the human rights and legal communities also criticized the president's "trial by television."

the assassin to and from the scene at the behest of D'Aubuisson associate Rafael Alvaro Saravia. Garay, who was located by U.S. and Salvadoran officials working with the U.S.-funded Special Investigative Unit, also swore that he overheard Savaria reporting back to D'Aubuisson that the mission was accomplished. According to Garay, D'Aubuisson responded that Saravia had acted too soon, while Saravia replied that he had done as D'Aubuisson had ordered.

Based on Garay's testimony, Salvadoran authorities issued an extradition request against Saravia, who was living in Miami. Saravia was arrested pending the outcome of extradition proceedings before U.S. Magistrate Linnea Johnson, U.S. District Court for the Southern District of Florida.

Saravia's lawyers in Miami argued against Saravia's extradition, claiming that Garay was a knowing participant in the crime and therefore legally incompetent to testify against Saravia under Salvadoran legal provisions that prevent accomplices from testifying against others implicated in the same crime.[27] The attorneys submitted a Salvadoran administrative judge's ruling on a habeas corpus petition brought on Saravia's behalf, which declared on these and other grounds that Garay's testimony was insufficient to hold Saravia on murder charges.[28] The Salvadoran judge's non-binding advisory opinion was submitted to the Salvadoran Supreme Court, which dismissed the extradition proceeding in December 1988.[29]

Salvadoran judicial and U.S. government sources express suspicion about the manner in which the administrative judge's

---

[27]Criminal Procedure Code, Articles 499 (3a) and 499-A. Guidelines on how to evaluate the credibility of testimony are specified in Articles 497 and 498 of the same code.

[28]"Respondent's Supplemental Pre-Hearing Memorandum in Opposition to Extradition," pp. 3-7. In re: Extradition of Alvaro Rafael Saravia Case No. 87-3598-Civ.

[29]See Miami Herald, January 13, 1989 and Washington Post, December 29, 1988. The Supreme Court ruled on a habeas petition filed in Saravia's behalf on July 18, 1988, saying there were no grounds to arrest him if he returned to El Salvador. In habeas petitions of this nature (known as a Recurso de Exhibicion Personal), the Supreme Court appoints an acting judge from the bar, known as a juez ejecutor.

opinion made its way to Miami *before* the Salvadoran Supreme Court obtained a copy. According to Supreme Court President Francisco Jose Guerrero, the early disclosure violates Salvadoran rules concerning judicial procedure.[30] U.S. sources told the Lawyers Committee that the opinion was sent to Miami on a FAX machine in the offices of Roberto D'Aubuisson.

While Saravia's lawyers prepared an appeal of Magistrate Johnson's September 1988 ruling that he should be extradited, the Salvadoran Supreme Court ruled in December 1988 that Saravia's extradition order was procedurally defective and could not stand. Saravia was soon freed on bail from a federal detention facility. The high court also ruled that Garay's testimony was too old and contradicted that of other witnesses.

In late December, the ARENA majority in the legislature voted -- with other parties abstaining -- to oust Attorney General Roberto Giron Flores for incompetence and fraud in the Romero and other cases. Among the charges against Giron Flores, Deputy Roberto D'Aubuisson asserted that the Attorney General had conceded in a closed-door session that Antonio Garay was actually a false witness.[31] In a Lawyers Committee interview, Giron Flores emphatically denied the charge, accusing D'Aubuisson and ARENA presidential candidate Alfredo Cristiani of deliberately distorting his remarks. Giron Flores said he had told the legislators that another individual -- who was detained on unrelated charges and had made jailhouse claims of knowledge about Romero's killers -- was clearly lying.[32]

Saravia's arrest rekindled interest in a diary captured at the time of the 1980 arrest of Roberto D'Aubuisson on charges of planning a coup against the ruling junta. The diary, which lists the names of numerous suspected death squad associates, also contains entries believed by some to refer to plans for the Romero murder.

---

[30]Lawyers Committee interview with Francisco Jose Guerrero at the Supreme Court, September 14, 1988.

[31]*La Prensa Grafica*, December 23, 1988.

[32]Lawyers Committee interview, Roberto Giron Flores, January 11, 1989.

24

Salvadoran judicial officials say that the original of the diary has not been located despite the government's possession of it after its seizure.

Case Closed

Reacting to the dismissal of the extradition request, a State Department spokesman in Washington said on December 29, 1988:

We are concerned that Salvadoran judicial authorities vigorously pursue human rights cases regardless of the violator's political persuasion or institutional affiliation. We are still seeking a full explanation of the implications of the decision. We will direct our Embassy to indicate our strong dissatisfaction with the decision to the Salvadoran government.

Observing that the case only progresses during electoral campaigns, Dr. Ricardo A. Zamora of San Salvador's Fourth Penal Court told the Lawyers Committee in January 1989 that the case is still open, based on the testimony -- recorded some four years ago -- of a nun who saw the gunmen drive off. The new Attorney General, Dr. Roberto Garcia Alvarado, said in early January that "The assassination of Msgr. Oscar Arnulfo Romero is not closed as the Church and the Department of State of the United States have expressed."[33] But by ruling that Garay's evidence is too old, the Supreme Court has set a precedent for courts to throw out later testimony in the case on the same grounds.

The Denouement

On February 5 and 7, 1989, the Salvadoran Government preempted television programming on all stations to air two videotapes laying out its case against Roberto D'Aubuisson, whom they named the intellectual author of the crime; Rafael Alvaro Saravia, who they say planned the killing; and Dr. Antonio Hector Regalado, who they named for the first time publicly as the triggerman. Known as "Dr. Death," Regalado is the dentist from Santiago de Maria who in the early 1980's ran his own death squad

---

[33]*La Prensa Grafica*, January 4, 1989.

25

disguised as a boy scout troop.[34] According to the videotape, Garay chose Regalado from among the sketches of three men, identifying him as the man he knew to have shot the Archbishop.

The government's case is built on evidence collected by the Special Investigative Unit; this evidence was turned over to the court on February 10.

The new Attorney General summoned Justice Minister Julio Alfredo Samayoa, former Attorney General Roberto Giron Flores, and the Vice Minister of Communications to make statements to the court, and subpoenaed the videotape.

On February 10 and 12, ARENA purchased television time to present two 45-minute videotapes in which Roberto D'Aubuisson emphatically rejected the goverment's accusations.

On February 24, Justice Minister Julio Alfredo Samayoa requested that the Legislative Assembly hold pre-trial hearings on the involvement of Roberto D'Aubuisson in the murder of Archbishop Romero. Before D'Aubuisson could stand trial the Assembly would have to find just cause, and strip him of his parliamentary immunity.[35]

---

[34]*The Washington Post*, August 29, 1988. Regalado, once D'Aubuisson's personal security advisor, is believed by U.S. authorities to be behind the spring 1984 plot to kill U.S. Ambassador Thomas Pickering. See Craig Pyes and Laurie Becklund, "Inside Dope in El Salvador," *The New Republic*, April 15, 1985.

[35]*El Mundo*, February 24, 1989; Radio Cadena YSU, February 24, 1989, as cited in FBIS LAT-89-040, March 2, 1989.

B. MASSACRE OF PEASANTS AT THE LAS HOJAS FARMING COOPERATIVE
February 22, 1983

The Massacre

On February 22, 1983, some 70 Indian peasants who belonged to the Las Hojas agricultural cooperative were killed by soldiers guided by masked members of the local civil defense.[36] Approximately 200 men attached to Military Outpost #6 at Sonsonate[37] were said to have arrived in three trucks in the early morning hours. According to witnesses, the soldiers dragged men from their homes and shot seven in the head. Reportedly, the names of these men were on an Army list of subversives.[38] Some 18 corpses were found in one location along a riverbank; all were shot at close range.

According to the National Association of Indigenous Salvadorans (ANIS), to which the victims belonged, the killings followed a property dispute. The owner of adjacent land had unsuccessfully sought right of way across the cooperative.

Gen. Jose Guillermo Garcia, then Defense Minister, pledged to investigate and prosecute the killers. Provisional President Alvaro Magana promised the victims' families $25,000 in indemnity.[39] And in 1984, newly elected President Duarte included the massacre among five human rights cases to be given special attention.

---

[36]See *Justice Denied: A Report on Twelve Unresolved Human Rights Cases in El Salvador* (Lawyers Committee for Human Rights, March 1985) pp. 56-61; and *El Salvador: Human Rights Dismissed, Report on 16 Unresolved Cases* (Lawyers Committee for Human Rights, 1986) pp. 49-53.

[37]One account said the soldiers belonged to the U.S.-trained Jaguar Battalion. *Dallas Morning News*, February 24, 1985.

[38]See *Human Rights Dismissed*, p. 50.

[39]*Dallas Morning News*, February 24, 1985.

The Aftermath

Court documents in the case cite three military men for responsibility for the killings: Major Oscar Alberto Leon Linares, Captain Carlos Alfonso Figueroa Morales, and Col. Elmer Gonzalez Araujo, then commander of the Sonsonate Garrison. Captain Figueroa, charged with responsibility for the murders by the governmental Human Right Commission, was cleared of any misconduct by his superiors and subsequently placed in charge of intelligence at the Sonsonate Garrison.[40]

Col. Araujo was later named to head the Armed Forces procurement office.[41] In 1986, a Virginia defense contractor who did a lucrative business with the Salvadoran military, pleaded guilty to paying nearly $400,000 in bribes to high-ranking Salvadoran military officials, among them Col. Araujo. According to one account of the scandal, "The contract was paid for by the U.S. government through a special foreign-aid loan program."[42]

An investigation by U.S. Embassy officials determined that troops under Col. Araujo's command were implicated in the killings. As a result, U.S. military advisors were withdrawn from the garrison.[43] Still on active duty, Gonzalez Araujo is currently in charge of another military purchasing unit, the *Intendencia de las Fuerzas Armadas.*

The Amnesty

On July 18, 1988, the Salvadoran Supreme Court upheld the amnesty granted by a lower court, citing Article 1 of the October

---

[40]*El Salvador: Human Rights Dismissed* (Lawyers Committee, 1986) p.51.

[41]Col. Araujo served as president of the *Comision de Compras de la Fuerza Armada*, headquartered in the Ministry of Defense.

[42]For a thorough report on the Nordac affair, see *The Virginian-Pilot and the Ledger-Star*, November 16, 1986. See also *Washington Post*, July 23 and September 27, 1986.

[43]Raymond Bonner, *Weakness and Deceit: U.S. Policy and El Salvador* (New York, 1984) pp.357-358.

1987 amnesty decree.[44] According to Article 1, forgiveness may be granted to direct or indirect participants in crimes and accomplices for political crimes, or common crimes associated with political crimes, or common crimes when they are committed by 20 or more persons before October 22, 1987.[45]

The Supreme Court's ruling affirms that there was no combat or guerrillas operating in the area at the time of massacre, in contrast to a version of events put forth by some officers. The decision dismissed charges against 14 members of the Armed Forces and civil defense, ruling that the 20-or-more rule was applicable even though only 14 participants were definitely identified.

In January 1989, a challenge to the Supreme Court ruling was filed with the Inter-American Commission on Human Rights of the Organization of American States.[46] Given that all domestic remedies on the case have been exhausted, the petitioners are asking the Inter-American Commission to investigate the massacre; to condemn the government of El Salvador for violating internationally recognized human rights standards and treaties to which it is a party; and for reparations for the families and ANIS. The challenge is still pending before the Inter-American Commission on Human Rights.

---

[44]Sala de lo Penal de la Corte Suprema de Justicia, San Salvador, July 18, 1988.

[45]Decree No. 805, Legislative Assembly of the Republic of El Salvador, October 27, 1987.

[46]The challenge was filed jointly by El Rescate and the Harvard Human Rights Program in cooperation with ANIS and the nongovernmental Human Rights Commission of El Salvador.

C. RODOLFO VIERA, MICHAEL HAMMER, AND MARK DAVID PEARLMAN
January 3, 1981
The Sheraton Murders

The Killings

Rodolfo Viera, president of the Salvadoran Agrarian Transformation Institute (ISTA), Michael Hammer, and Mark David Pearlman, both U.S. land reform advisors working for the AFL-CIO's American Institute of Free Labor Development (AIFLD), were murdered on January 3, 1981 as they were dining at San Salvador's elite Sheraton Hotel.[47]

Also in the hotel coffee shop late that evening were two wealthy Salvadoran businessmen, Ricardo Sol Meza and Hans Christ, co-owners of the Sheraton. Joining them at dinner were three Salvadoran military officers: Major Mario Denis Moran, Lt. Isidro Lopez Sibrian, and Captain Eduardo Ernesto Alfonso Avila, all close associates of ARENA founder Roberto D'Aubuisson, himself a former officer. According to the testimonies of two National Guardsmen who were serving as bodyguards to the officers, Lopez Sibrian and Avila spotted the land reform officials and ordered the guardsmen to kill them.

The Convictions

The confessed triggermen, National Guard Corporals Santiago Gomez Gonzalez and Jose Dimas Valle Acevedo, were convicted in February 1986, receiving a 30-year prison term, the maximum possible under Salvadoran law.

Though both men named Avila and Lopez Sibrian as the intellectual authors of the crime, their testimony could not be submitted in court because under Salvadoran law the testimony of one person implicated in a crime is not valid against another charged with the same crime. Lopez Sibrian, dismissed from the Army, was granted a "definite stay of proceedings" in the case by the Supreme Court in November 1984. Since 1986, Lopez Sibrian

---

[47]See *Human Rights Dismissed*, pp. 17-27. This earlier Lawyers Committee report describes in detail the case's six-year journey through the justice system.

has been jailed in connection with a kidnapping-for-profit ring. Charges against him were dropped and his release ordered on March 31, 1989. Responding to protest from Washington, ARENA, and the businessmen's association (ANEP), that order was quickly reversed on April 3, and Lopez Sibrian remains in detention.

Capt. Avila, also cashiered, was detained in December 1983, apparently in response to pressure brought to bear by then Vice-President George Bush during his celebrated visit to El Salvador that month.[48] Yet murder charges were not brought, and Avila was only charged with abandoning his military post without permission. He was released in March 1984, though the murder case against him remained open. Avila's uncle, Dr. Ricardo Avila Moriera, a founder of the right-wing ARENA party, is a Supreme Court Justice.

Ricardo Sol Meza was arrested in April 1981 and the government attempted to extradite Hans Christ from Miami, where he had sought refuge from the law. That August, a Salvadoran judge dismissed the cases against the two men on the grounds that there was insufficient evidence. That decision was upheld by an appeals court in April 1982 and again by the Supreme Court that July, thereby dismissing all charges against the two businessmen. Hans Christ was represented in the extradition case by the same Miami law firm which defended Rafael Alvaro Saravia, implicated in the murder of Archbishop Romero.

The Investigation

As one of President Duarte's five priority cases, the Sheraton murders were referred to the Commission on Investigations in 1985. In October 1985 a Commission member indicated to Lawyers Committee representatives that the investigation would continue. In *Human Rights Dismissed* we wrote that the Commission considered:

> the case of substantial 'symbolic' value because 'national honor is at stake' and 'the union [the AFL-CIO] is constantly pressing for action.' He also asserted that 'Avila will be prosecuted.' Nonetheless, there are no signs that the Commission has

---

[48]See *Human Rights Dismissed*, p. 21.

undertaken any serious investigation into the involvement of higher-ups in the murders.[49]

According to a list of crimes investigated by the Special Investigative Unit, the Commission's investigatory body, the case is now closed; the list states simply that the triggermen were granted amnesty.[50]

The Amnesty

On December 11, 1987, Fifth Penal Judge Rosa Maria Fortin granted amnesty to the convicted triggermen and Captain Avila. In explaining her decision the Judge said:

It is my finding that this crime fits the legal definition of political crime and therefore falls under the amnesty enacted November 5. If the purpose of the killings was to end the land reform, it was political and if it was to kill a government official, it is also political.[51]

The decision was immediately appealed by the Attorney General with the backing of the U.S. Embassy.

An appellate court upheld the ruling on December 19 and the men were freed that same day, just hours before the three-week Christmas recess began. Citing court sources, *The Washington Post* wrote that this "maneuver was made...in an attempt to mitigate the ruling's impact in the United States."[52] The AFL-CIO, the State Department, and the U.S. Embassy -- which said it first learned of the finding from accounts in the local press -- had all pursued the case more forcefully than most over the years.

---

[49]*Human Rights Dismissed*, pp.17-18.

[50]*Nomina de Casos Asignados a la Unidad Ejecutiva de la Comision de Investigacion de Hechos Delictivos.* See p. 41 for a discussion of the Special Investigative Unit.

[51]*The Washington Post*, December 15, 1987.

[52]*The Washington Post*, December 30, 1987.

32

The Reaction

In a prepared statement, a U.S. Embassy spokesman said:

We are appalled and outraged at the court's rejecting the government's appeal of the amnesty granted in this case, which was not in our view a political crime. The Sheraton case was tried as a common crime and the killers convicted under purely criminal statutes.[53]

Further, the Embassy threatened to cut U.S. aid to the Judicial Reform Program: "Given the situation, we plan to review the level and types of assistance we are providing to the Salvadoran judiciary." No action was ever taken on that threat.

In mid-1988, the U.S. Government granted Mark David Pearlman, who worked in El Salvador under an AID contract, status as a "protected person" under the Convention on the Prevention and Punishment of Crimes Against Internationally Protected Persons, Including Diplomatic Agents. On April 1, 1988, the State Department requested that El Salvador recognize this status for Pearlman posthumously, which the government did in a diplomatic note to the U.S. Embassy on December 9, 1988. This diplomatic note is now pending before the Salvadoran Supreme Court, according to a source at the U.S. Embassy. It is unclear what impact, if any, this will have on the case.

Despite the AFL-CIO's efforts to keep the case alive and the State Department's diplomatic initiative, there is little likelihood that further steps will be taken to pursue the intellectual authors of the crime.

After the triggermen were released from jail, a San Salvador daily wrote:

U.S. leftists cleverly exploited the Viera case by blaming Salvadoran businessmen for the crime and have tried to make them appear as advocates and backers of the so-called death squads. In this way, the Christian Democrats, whom the United States has

---

[53]*The Washington Post*, December 31, 1987.

been sponsoring for the past 10 years, would be made to appear as the only solution for El Salvador.[54]

---

[54]*El Diario de Hoy*, December 28, 1987, as cited in FBIS-LAT-87-249, December 29, 1987.

D. THE ARMENIA MASSACRE
July 30, 1981

The Killings

Between 19 and 41 members of the Las Lajas soccer team were killed on July 30, 1981 allegedly by soldiers, following a minor altercation between the players and men guarding a military roadblock.[55] Four days after the dispute, soldiers entered the town of Armenia at about 6:00 p.m. Residents were told to stay inside while a house-to-house search was conducted by the troops, who dragged people from their homes. Archbishop Arturo Rivera y Damas of San Salvador later denounced "the capture and subsequent murder of 23 people in Armenia on July 30."[56]

The Investigation

Armenia was the only one of President Duarte's five priority cases that was investigated by the Cestoni Commission.[57] Early efforts focussed on excavation of a dry well where some of the victims had been dumped. In order to proceed with prosecutions, Salvadoran law requires that the bodies be exhumed and the remains examined to determine cause of death. Almost four years after the deaths, an unsuccessful attempt was made to exhume the bodies in October 1984.

A 1985 Lawyers Committee delegation, which attempted to trace the development of the investigation and particularly plans for a second exhumation, was told "excuse after excuse for inaction. Many turned out to have no basis in fact."[58] In our 1987 study on El Salvador's judicial system we concluded: "The delegation is convinced that as late as the fall of 1985 little or nothing had been done to investigate the Armenia case."[59]

---

[55]See *Human Rights Dismissed*, pp.59-62.

[56]*The Washington Post*, August 17, 1981.

[57]For a discussion of the Cestoni Commission, the forerunner to the Commission on Investigations, see p.36.

[58]*From the Ashes*, p.21.

[59]*Ibid.*

35

The Case

Twenty soldiers and members of the civil defense were implicated in the crime. In 1985, the cases against several key defendants were dismissed, a decision that was overturned by the Western Appellate Penal Court in Santa Ana on March 20, 1986. The court also ordered that the well be excavated. A second exhumation was conducted on May 16, 1986, this time by the Commission on Investigations, to which the case had been referred. Witnesses say it was conducted in a professional manner, with the collaboration of the Fire Department, the Military Sanitation Unit, and the National Guard, among others. The remains of four people were exhumed in the presence of the media, human rights workers, and families hoping to identify missing relatives. Three victims were identified by name.

Eight men were originally detained in the case[60], and seven civil guardsmen remain jailed awaiting trial.[61] Eight years after the massacre, the case remains in the investigation phase in Armenia's First Instance Court. The men were denied amnesty, a ruling that was upheld on February 18, 1988 by the Santa Ana appellate court. Defense attorneys for the guardsmen have appealed the denial of amnesty to the Supreme Court, which, as of early April 1989, had not yet ruled in the matter.

---

[60]*Human Rights Dismissed*, p.62.

[61]"Report on the Situation in El Salvador," Pursuant to Section 561 of Public Law 100-202, December 1, 1988, Department of State, p. 4.

The exhumation at Tepemechin, Morazan, May 24, 1988.
(photo: Corinne Dufka)

CHAPTER II: JUDICIAL REFORM PROJECT (1984-1989)

In his inaugural address to the nation in June 1984, Salvadoran President Jose Napoleon Duarte pledged to make respect for human rights a central focus of his administration. Referring explicitly to the killings in 1980 of Archbishop Oscar Arnulfo Romero and the four U.S. churchwomen, as well as several other notorious cases from the early 1980's, President Duarte emphasized:

> I will fight openly and tirelessly to control abuses of authority and violence of the extremes.

In August of that year, Duarte appointed a special commission to investigate political killings. The commission was charged with investigating five well-publicized human rights cases, including the murder of Archbishop Romero, the Las Hojas and Armenia massacres, and the killing of the two U.S. land reform advisors and their Salvadoran colleague.

President Duarte's actions signalled his recognition that the Salvadoran government's failure to prosecute these celebrated cases and others seriously undermined the rule of law in his country. He also acknowledged the need to devise institutional measures to revitalize a crippled judicial system.

The Commission he established was known as the Cestoni Commission, for its chairman Dr. Benjamin Cestoni.[62] During the year it existed, the Commission conducted only one inquiry -- of the Armenia well case -- and failed even in its efforts to advance that investigation.

By the summer of 1985, the Cestoni Commission had given way to the Commission on Investigations. According to a senior Salvadoran government official quoted in *The New York Times*, the Cestoni Commission was "dismantled without achieving any of its objectives."[63] Further, *The Times* reported:

---

[62]Dr. Benjamin Cestoni heads the governmental Human Rights Commission (CDH), a project of AID's Office of Democratic Initiatives. The CDH is slated to receive $300,000 in FY 88-89 out of local currency funds.

[63]*The New York Times*, November 23, 1985.

Some of Mr. Duarte's critics inside the Government and in the Roman Catholic Church said they believed that human rights investigations had been used as a propaganda issue. According to senior judiciary officials, the special presidential commission rarely met, took few steps and recently handed over its "meager" files to the new investigative body.

With the Cestoni Commission gone, a group of military investigators began to work informally under the leadership of Lt. Col. Joel Rivas and Major Carlos Aviles.[64] These detectives, who concentrated their efforts on a ring of car thieves and illegal foreign adoptions of Salvadoran babies,[65] were subsumed into the Commission on Investigations. A Commission employee told *The New York Times* in November 1985 that the:

new group switched to politically less sensitive problems...because it was decided it was too weak to take on the murder cases, which apparently involved military officers, soldiers, and in some instances influential citizens.

One reason given for the failure of the Cestoni Commission was a lack of funds.[66] In late 1984, the United States Government initiated a grant program designed to resuscitate El Salvador's system of justice, including its capacity to investigate political crimes.

The agreement was signed by President Duarte and the Agency for International Development (AID) in July 1984 and was

---

[64]In April 1985, a Lawyers Committee representative was told by Major Aviles that his training to head the SIU began as early as February 1984.

[65]Interview with Carlos Aviles, who served as Executive Officer and later Commanding Officer of the SIU and chief of the Armed Forces press office, COPREFA, Estado Mayor, June 1985.

[66]See *From the Ashes*, p. 14. The Americas Watch reported in 1985 that the ARENA-controlled Constituent Assembly provided no funding for the Commission and that out-of-pocket expenses were covered by the office of the Presidency. See *Draining the Sea...* (Americas Watch, March 1985) pp. 67-69.

ratified by the Legislative Assembly in August.[67] The agreement had two components: the Legislative Revisory Commission and the Judicial Protection Unit. In May 1985, the agreement was amended and immediately approved by the Assembly to cover two additional components: the Commission on Investigations and Judicial Administration and Training.

Since FY 1984, $9.2 million from AID has been earmarked for El Salvador and $5.1 million from the Government of El Salvador for a total of $14.3 million.[68] In FY 1988, the program was granted an additional $1 million which was not spent. In FY 1989, the AID Mission in San Salvador plans to request $4 million in additional funding for the Judicial Reform Program. If, as expected, that request is approved, total direct U.S. funding for the Salvadoran judicial system since 1985 will have totalled $14.2 million.

Administration of Justice in Latin America and the Caribbean

El Salvador's Judicial Reform Program is part of a $20 million regional effort in the Caribbean and Latin America known as the Administration of Justice Program. (AOJ).[69] In addition to El Salvador, more than 10 Latin American and Caribbean countries are currently participating in AOJ programs.[70]

---

[67]*CORELESAL-Informa*, March 1988, no.4, p.10.

[68]In FY 1984, $3 million was earmarked and in FY 1985 an additional $6 million was added. The total $9.2 million allocation for El Salvador from FY 1984 to FY 1988 does not come out of regional allocations. But as of June 1988, under $3 million of the U.S. portion had been spent with the remaining $6.5 million in U.S. aid committed but not expended.

[69]Between 1984 and 1987, Congress granted over $36 million for the AOJ program in Latin America and the Caribbean. In FY 1988 and 1989, AOJ was earmarked at $20 million annually.

[70]Costa Rica, El Salvador, Guatemala, Honduras; Jamaica and the islands of the Eastern Caribbean; Argentina (not yet authorized), Bolivia, Chile, Colombia, Peru. Planning is underway to take the Administration of Justice Program to countries in other parts of the world, such as the Philippines.

Inspired by the recommendations of the 1984 Kissinger Commission on Central America, statutory authority for AOJ was provided by a 1985 amendment to the Foreign Assistance Act.[71] AOJ monies may be allocated to "countries and organizations, including national and regional institutions, in order to strengthen the administration of justice in countries in Latin America and the Caribbean. Assistance under this section may only include:[72]

1. support for specialized professional training, scholarships and exchanges for continuing legal education;

2. programs to enhance prosecutorial and judicial capabilities and protection for participants in judicial cases;

3. notwithstanding section 660 of this Act[73]

(A) programs to enhance professional capabilities to carry out investigative and forensic functions conducted under judicial or prosecutorial control;

(B) programs to assist in the development of academic instruction and curricula for training law enforcement personnel;

(C) programs to improve the administrative and management capabilities relating to career development, personnel evaluation, and internal discipline procedures; and

(D) programs, conducted through multilateral or regional institutions, to improve penal institutions and the rehabilitation of offenders;

---

[71]Section 534 of the Foreign Assistance Act of 1961.

[72]Section 534 of the Foreign Assistance Act of 1961, as amended in 1985 and again in late 1987.

[73]Section 660 prohibits police training.

41

4. strengthening professional organizations in order to promote services to members and the role of the bar in judicial selection, enforcement of ethical standards, and legal reform;

5. increasing the availability of legal materials and publications;

6. seminars, conferences, and training and educational programs to improve the administration of justice and to strengthen respect for the rule of law and internationally recognized human rights; and

7. revision and modernization of legal codes and procedures.

The AOJ program also finances police training through the International Criminal Assistance and Training Program (ICITAP), which allows for U.S. training of foreign police forces despite the blanket ban passed in 1974.[74] Of the $20 million yearly total for AOJ, not more than $7 million may be spent on ICITAP. In FY 1988, ICITAP's authority was expanded and its funding more than doubled, for a regional total of $6.4 million, some $700,000 of which was slated for El Salvador.

---

[74]Legislative authority for police training through the Administration of Justice Program is contained in Section 534(b)(3). For a discussion of ICITAP and other programs training Salvadoran police, see Chapter IV.

A. COMMISSION ON INVESTIGATIONS

With $5.5 million in funding since 1985, the Commission on Investigations[75] is the most expensive and in many ways the most important component of El Salvador's Judicial Reform Program.[76] In our view, it has been the least successful. In FY 1988 and FY 1989, an additional $1.2 million is slated to be channeled to the Commission.

Created by Decree No. 58 of July 4, 1985, the Commission was established, according to AID, "to develop criminal investigation capabilities, supported by crime laboratory facilities, so that the courts will have access to impartial evidentiary materials and expert testimony which are needed to apply the law and impart justice effectively."[77]

The three-member Commission on Investigations consists of Justice Minister Julio Alfredo Samayoa, who serves as chairman; Vice-Minister of the Interior Carmen Amelia Barahona de Morales; and former Economy Minister Ricardo Perdomo, the designate of President Duarte.[78] The Commission has a full-time Executive Secretary, Dr. Carcamo Quintana, who also has his own law practice.[79] Dr. Quintana described his role in trafficking cases, acting as liaison between the Commission and the government. His

---

[75]The Commission on Investigations is known in Spanish as the *Comision de Investigacion de Hechos Delictivos.*

[76]The Commission was originally granted $3.5 million in U.S. funding plus $2 million in Salvadoran counterpart funds generated by Economic Support Funds donated by the United States. As of June 30, 1988, approximately $1.5 million had been expended and another $3 million committed.

[77]"El Salvador: Judicial Reform Program," Agency for International Development, March 17, 1988.

[78]The Commission's membership is specified in Article 2 of the *Ley de Creacion de la Comision de Investigacion de Hechos Delictivos,* July 4, 1985.

[79]Lawyers Committee interview with Dr. Carcamo Quintana, July 7, 1988.

staff numbers six and he said he was not involved in the cases and had practically no contact with the detectives.

Nominally, the Commission is the parent organization of an Executive Unit, headed by two colonels, who in turn oversee the work of a Special Investigative Unit (SIU) and a Forensic Laboratory (known as the FU). When necessary, the two units may seek the counsel of a Legal Advisor also serving under the Commission.[80] According to Dr. Quintana, the staff of the Executive Unit numbers 109.

The Special Investigative Unit consists of between 25 and 30 detectives, all drawn from the Security Forces, which continue to provide the detectives' base salary. As active duty members of the Security Forces, the investigators are subject to military discipline and dependent on the military for career advancement and retirement benefits. All three of the country's main police corps are under the command of the Ministry of Defense.

This apparent conflict of interest has drawn criticism from human rights groups and other observers within El Salvador as well as internationally. Since the unit is charged with investigating the most sensitive human rights cases -- in which military men and powerful civilians are often implicated -- the chances of it being able to conduct an impartial investigation are slim. SIU commanders are all career officers who are assigned to the unit as a rotation within their military service. Given the military's tight-knit structure, it is not realistic to expect an SIU officer to rigorously pursue investigations that could lead to the highest levels of the Armed Forces, potentially rocking the institution to its foundations. An outside team commissioned by AID to evaluate the project found that this revolving door between the military and the SIU "substantially [affects] the image of the SIU and FU in the eyes of many...."[81]

---

[80]The SIU is known in Spanish as the *Unidad de Investigaciones*. The Forensic Laboratory is known as the *Unidad Tecnica Forense* and the legal office is the *Asesoria Juridica*.

[81]Evaluation of the Judicial Reform Project, No.519-0296, USAID/El Salvador," Arthur Mudge, Team Leader, Steve Flanders, Miguel Sanchez, Adolfo Saenz, and Gilberto Trujillo, Final Report, March 1988, p.13.

This presents a seeming contradiction in that a principal reason for establishing the SIU was lack of confidence in the capacity or willingness of the military-dominated police forces to investigate cases in which military complicity was suspected.

The explanation for this arrangement is that Article 11 of the Criminal Procedure Code designates the three Security Forces as "auxiliary organs" of the court. Only evidence gathered by auxiliary organs is admissible in judicial proceedings. Because the SIU lacks this status, its findings can only be submitted to the courts if its detectives are members of an institution already designated as an auxiliary organ. As the evaluators contracted by AID rightfully concluded: "such legal impediment is hardly insuperable. We understand that the current situation is a matter of political will, and of power balance between the civilian government and the military."[82]

The Forensic Laboratory

U.S. policymakers argue that essential to any meaningful reform of El Salvador's justice system is an acceptance of the role of scientific forensic evidence in criminal investigations. El Salvador's system is heavily weighted toward the confession, giving rise to torture and other coercive methods in the attempt to extract an admission of guilt.

In response, the Judicial Reform Program included the construction of a forensic laboratory, for which some $1.7 million in U.S. aid was budgeted. AID reports an extensive list of training courses offered to the unit's 25 technicians, exceeding the budgeted staff number by 15. Personnel have been trained in the United States and Costa Rica as well as in El Salvador in fingerprinting, ballistics, document examination, polygraphing, photography, serology, hairs and fiber analysis, chemistry, toxology, and minerology.

From the outset, the laboratory drew criticism because of its placement within the military compound housing the High Command. In defending the decision, an AID official said the High Command was the "only place available that could provide the

---

[82]Mudge, *et al.*, p.14.

necessary security."[83] In response to criticism that witnesses who were forced to pass a military check point might be dissuaded from delivering evidence to the lab, the official said that "witnesses had no reason to go to the lab."

Further, the same official said that a U.S. advisor attached to the laboratory "never felt any pressure by being on the grounds" of the High Command. "I've heard of no cases of intimidation. Alleged intimidation does not exist," he insisted.

AID's evaluation team did not agree:

> The location of the Forensic Laboratory in the military compound impairs its usefulness. The limitations are both practical, in discouraging access of judges and other civilians involved in cases, and political in further indicating military domination of the SIU and the FU investigative functions.[84]

Further, they said that locating the lab some distance from the SIU "does not encourage or facilitate close working relationships...."

After much discussion, a home for the laboratory has been found. Permanent quarters for the lab are to be built within the new police academy outside San Salvador on the road to Santa Tecla.[85] This facility should be completed by early 1990, though work has been halted pending the outcome of a dispute over title to the land.

Not all U.S. officials find the hefty price tag worth it. One Embassy official confided to us: "We've put $1.5 million into the Forensic Lab and I haven't seen a dime's worth of difference in the fact that it's there."[86]

---

[83]Lawyers Committee interview, AID, San Salvador, May 23, 1988.

[84]Mudge, et al., p.16.

[85]According to AID's most recent status report on the Judicial Reform Program, the Commission on Investigations and the Vice-Ministry for Public Security -- which oversees the country's police -- have both agreed to the change.

[86]Lawyers Committee interview, U.S. Embassy, September 1988.

A Training Twist

Detectives attached to the SIU have also been through extensive training, initially by the FBI in 1984 in Puerto Rico. According to AID, in the last six months they have studied "high visibility homicide; criminal intelligence; the use of informants; and advanced interview techniques." Planned in the next six months are "major case management; firearms training; white collar crimes; and hostage negotiations." The U.S. advisor to the unit is a retired member of the U.S. military.

The extensive U.S. financing and involvement in the SIU and the laboratory also raise serious questions about prohibitions on police training. According to current U.S. law, all police training is prohibited. By training SIU detectives and technicians at the forensic lab, the government is in effect circumventing this ban. In fact, according to the Mudge study, the SIU was established as a separate unit to avoid raising eyebrows about U.S. police training:

> The separate unit was established at U.S. insistence actually, in order to avoid raising questions under U.S. statutes restricting assistance to military and police units. Further, such independence might help insulate investigations from military pressure in cases where the military was suspected of acts of complicity.[87]

There is little evidence that the unit has been "insulated" from military pressure.

Case Selection Criteria

What the evaluators deemed "purposely flexible criteria" for the selection of cases to be investigated is, in our view, so vague as to ensure arbitrary and politicized decision-making.[88] Article One of the law creating the Commission mandates it to "study, classify and order the investigation of all those criminal acts which, by their nature, by the persons involved as victims or authors of the

---

[87]Mudge, *et al.*, pp.48-49.

[88]Mudge and his colleagues found that "the Commission appears responsive to current needs in selection of cases. We do not see need for further definition of the current purposely flexible criteria...." (p. 18).

crime, by the means employed to execute the crime, or by their impact on the government or public opinion, have grave repercussions for the public and social order of the country."[89]

Articles Five and Six mandate the civilian Commission to meet weekly to determine which cases should be tackled, ordering the SIU to investigate when appropriate.[90] According to Article Eight, the SIU may launch an investigation on its own between weekly meetings, within 72 hours notifying the Commission, which may approve or suspend the inquiry.

"The law doesn't spell out which cases to take up," Justice Minister Samayoa told us. "There's a wide spectrum."[91] An AID official acknowledged that "it's a political decision which cases are investigated."[92] A Salvadoran judge offered, "The SIU only takes up cases which interest them."[93]

In practice, we found the decision-making confused and the case selection poor. The Commission seems to take little initiative in pursuing controversial cases. When asked why the SIU had not looked into the Soyapango sand-digger killings, Dr. Samayoa replied, "No one asked us to. We don't get in if we're not asked."[94] The Justice Minister's explanation flies in the face of case selection

---

[89]*Ley de Creacion de la Comision de Investigacion de Hechos Delictivos*, July 4, 1985, Article One.

[90]While only the three civilian Commission members enjoy voting rights, also attending the weekly meetings are the Secretary General of the Commission, currently Dr. Carcamo Quintana, and the chief of the Executive Unit, currently Col. Nelson Ivan Lopez y Lopez, who briefs the group about investigations in progress. See Article Four of the *Reglamento Especial de la Ley de Creacion de la Comision de Investigacion de Hechos Delictivos*.

[91]Lawyers Committee interview with Justice Minister Julio Alfredo Samayoa, SIU headquarters, San Salvador, July 15, 1988.

[92]Lawyers Committee interview, AID, San Salvador, May 23, 1988.

[93]Lawyers Committee interview, San Salvador, October 1988.

[94]Lawyers Committee interview with Dr. Samayoa, July 15, 1988. On the sand-digger deaths, see p. 108.

procedures which he himself had described earlier, as well as that specified by the enabling legislation.

The law says that cases which touch "the national conscience" or have "grave repercussions" for society should be taken up as a matter of course. Yet in 1988 the SIU failed to investigate two very troubling human rights cases: the *Puerta del Diablo* killings and the San Francisco massacre. The Attorney General's office told the Lawyers Committee that because it lacked the necessary investigative capacity, it had asked the SIU to investigate *Puerta del Diablo*. Yet when we asked about the unit's investigation, Justice Minister Samayoa told us no inquiry had been ordered.

Nor did the Commission feel compelled to launch an investigation last September of the massacre of 10 peasants at San Francisco, San Vicente. When the bodies were exhumed with uncharacteristic timeliness just two weeks after the murders, the SIU failed to respond to requests to participate. When a Lawyers Committee representative asked a judicial official at the grave site why the SIU was not there, we were told the court had been unable to meet the unit's security requirements and that there was not sufficient lead-time.[95]

A U.S. Embassy official later asserted that the SIU failed to act because President Duarte, who he said determines the SIU docket, had not ordered them to do so. A State Department report to Congress said that President Duarte finally ordered the inquiry in late October,[96] yet according to Embassy reports, work did not get underway until mid-January. More than anything, the SIU appeared spurred to action by mounting pressure on the military

---

[95]The official did not indicate from whom the SIU felt it needed protection. Soldiers of the Fifth Brigade, the unit charged with the killings, hovered over the proceedings all day and military helicopters swooped in several times over the gravesites, low enough that those on the ground could see the pilots' faces.

[96]"Report on the Situation in El Salvador," December 1, 1988, pursuant to Section 561 of Public Law 100-202.

from Washington, which culminated in the February 3 visit of Vice-President Dan Quayle.

In late March 1989, the Lawyers Committee learned of a secret agreement allegedly made one year ago between President Duarte and Defense Minister Vides Casanova. Under the reported unwritten accord, the SIU may not launch investigations of crimes in which the Armed Forces are implicated unless Duarte orders the unit to do so, presumably after discussion with the Defense Minister. The Lawyers Committee is greatly disturbed by the revelation of this agreement, which severely undermines any notion of SIU independence.

The Portfolio Profile

In *From the Ashes*, we wrote, "Despite this air of activity, human rights cases seem to have been relegated to the lowest rung on the Commission's priority ladder."[97] Lamentably, nothing we have learned since has changed that view.

At our request, the Justice Minister provided a list of SIU cases: 42 closed; 13 suspended; and 14 active, for a total of 69.[98]

---

[97]*From the Ashes*, p.19.

[98]While the list was described as complete, we later learned of investigations not listed, and heard estimates of a total caseload ranging from 35 to 90. Further, some on the list were not officially SIU cases, such as the Zona Rosa killings, which occurred in June 1985, some two months before the SIU got off the ground, and the kidnapping of President Duarte's daughter in September 1985.
In both the Zona Rosa and the Duarte kidnapping, the SIU played supporting roles to the investigations conducted by the Security Forces. Secretary General Carcamo Quintana told the Lawyers Committee on July 7, 1988 that only technical forensic assistance was provided for these two investigations. President Duarte praised the police's investigation of the Zona Rosa killings. The three suspects, who later said their confessions resulted from psychological and physical torture, remain jailed almost four years after their detention and have never been tried. See *Waiting for Justice: Treatment of Political Prisoners Under El Salvador's Decree 50* (International Human Rights Law Group, March 1987) pp.64-65. See also *From the Ashes*, pp. 16-19.
AID's evaluators observed that by "U.S. standards this is not a heavy caseload [67 cases between July 1985 and September 1987]."

Of President Duarte's five priority cases, supposedly forming the initial core of the SIU's portfolio, only the investigation into the murder of Archbishop Romero remains active; inquiries into the Sheraton killings, the Armenia well deaths, and the disappearance of U.S. journalist John Sullivan had all been closed by July 1988. The Las Hojas massacre, amnestied by the Supreme Court last July, does not appear on the roster.[99]

Of the 14 active investigations, only four can definitely be termed human rights cases; two additional cases may involve human rights violations; the remaining eight are cases involving common crimes and corruption.

Of the 42 closed investigations, 15 are human rights cases. The FMLN took responsibility for two; and in a third, the SIU implicated the rebel movement in the 1987 murder of human rights activist Herbert Anaya. The Armed Forces are implicated in six of these 15 cases.

Two additional cases may involve human rights violations. Assuming that they are, the total of 17 human rights cases still comprises under half the total portfolio of closed investigations.

Of the 13 suspended inquiries, seven are human rights violations. Members of the military or Civil Defense are implicated in six out of these seven suspended cases.

Of a total portfolio of 69 cases, 26 are clearly human rights violations; 43 involve common crimes or corruption, while a few are listed for inexplicable reasons. In our view, this record is unacceptable for a Commission mandated to focus on human rights.

Mudge, *et al.*, p.11.

[99]Dr. Samayoa told the Lawyers Committee on September 14, 1988 that the U.S. Embassy had not provided necessary information concerning John Sullivan. At the end of last year, he said, the SIU had located Sullivan's suitcase -- checked at the Camino Real Hotel since his disappearance in 1980 -- containing personal documents and a camouflage uniform. The list of closed cases provided to the Lawyers Committee last July says the SIU did "not obtain all the necessary information from the victim's family." *Nomina de Casos Asignados a la Unidad Ejecutiva de la Comision de Investigacion de Hechos Delictivos.*

51

During the summer of 1988 when we conducted most of our research, the SIU was concentrating on corruption cases in which Christian Democratic politicians and government functionaries were implicated. In defending the SIU record, a high-ranking Embassy official told the Lawyers Committee that the unit "was gaining credibility by going after civilians as well as military, by going after high PDC people. I don't object to the investigations into car theft and adoption fraud. We can't expect them to only look into U.S. human rights cases."[100]

An AID official said if the "SIU only tackled human rights cases the military would think they were out after them, so they have to investigate everyone."[101] Another U.S. diplomat insisted that "no celebrated human rights cases had not been investigated."[102] Unfortunately, many "celebrated" human rights cases have obviously fallen through the cracks of the SIU's selection criteria.

In discussing the impact of the 1987 amnesty, the outside evaluating team seemed by inference to render the SIU meaningless:

> In view of the amnesty, it is entirely understandable that the investigation units would not give highest priority to tracking down perpetrators of likely "political" crimes only to see them freed under the amnesty. Particularly would this be so for a case in which military colleagues of SIU leadership were suspects. Assuming the SIU leadership had the integrity to risk military disfavor, they should hardly have been expected to do so pointlessly. During our stay in El Salvador the SIU quite logically was directing most of its resources at the two most important cases not covered by the amnesty -- the Romero and Anaya cases.[103]

---

[100]Lawyers Committee interview, U.S. Embassy, September 12, 1988.

[101]Lawyers Committee interview, AID, San Salvador, September 1988.

[102]Lawyers Committee interview, U.S. Embassy, San Salvador, September 12, 1988.

[103]Mudge, et al., pp.12-13.

The record is undistinguished. One notable example is the Romero case, repeatedly called an "SIU success story" by Embassy officials. Since this case was, in effect, wiped off the books in a blatantly partisan fashion, the SIU's "success" was rendered moot.

A Commission with No Authority

Since July 1987, the Commission has in fact been functioning under a dubious mandate. Article 14 of the authorizing legislation says that the Commission "shall be transitory and its objectives and results will be evaluated two years after its creation...by the Revisory Commission on Salvadoran Legislation," which should then make a recommendation on institutionalizing the project.

To our knowledge, CORELESAL[104] has never examined the Commission's record. "For various political reasons, it was decided not to make the decision," an AID official told the Lawyers Committee in May 1988. The official said the SIU had continued nonetheless, since Article 14 merely calls for the evaluation, stopping short of abolishing the Commission at the expiration of its mandate. In March 1989, another U.S. diplomat told the Lawyers Committee that since the ARENA-dominated Assembly was apt to oppose institutionalizing the SIU, "it was better not to raise the issue at all."

The question is further complicated by a U.S. decision to transfer authority for the Commission and the Judicial Protection Unit from AID to the State Department. This was done in order to relieve AID of any jurisdiction over police training and thereby avoid comparison with the discredited Office of Public Safety. Between 1962 and 1974, AID's Office of Public Safety ran an extensive police training program, placing approximately 400 "Public Safety Advisors" in some 52 countries.[105] In 1974, Congress ordered the office dissolved amidst allegations that trainees in countries such as Guatemala and Iran had engaged in torture.

---

[104]CORELESAL is an acronym for *Comision Revisora de la Legislacion Salvadorena.*

[105]See "Police Aid and Political Will: U.S. Policy in El Salvador and Honduras (1962-1987)," (Washington Office on Latin America, 1987), especially pp.4-17.

Implementation of this decision has been slow and, according to AID's most recent status report, "no final action has been taken." In the AID Mission's view, "This uncertainty in the status of this component has undermined long-term planning for the Commission."

An Assessment

In *From the Ashes*, we concluded that there is "little reason to think that the Special Investigative Unit or any other Salvadoran agency would ever do a thorough investigation into the perpetrators of the human rights abuses of the past."[106] Recent developments in two prominent early cases illustrate what can happen when these investigations are pursued. The SIU invested a lot of time and resources in the Romero investigation. It was the SIU that identified Garay, verified his truthfulness, located Saravia in Miami, and identifed Regalado as the gunman. An Embassy official told us, "There's mountains and mountains of evidence."[107]

We have no privileged information about their investigation or the strength of the case they have constructed, but we shall assume for the purposes of argument that their case is sound. In the end, good police work amounted to nothing, when their findings were invalidated by the machinations of compromised and politicized judicial and legislative branches of government.

And in the kidnapping-for-profit case -- often touted as an example of Salvadoran willingness to pursue criminals within the military -- Judge Serrano's integrity resulted in his death. When other attempts at influence fail, murder of those who stick their necks out for justice is still an option; accountability for such murders is not likely.

The SIU did not investigate the kidnapping-for-profit case. It has, though, been investigating the killing of Judge Jorge Alberto Serrano, who was in charge of the case. In July Commission Executive Secretary Carcamo Quintana told us that the SIU "was deeply into the case. There's lots of evidence." One week later Justice Minister Samayoa said that suspects had been identified among the associates of two military officers and a civilian who have been jailed in the kidnapping-for-profit case since 1986. By

---

[106]*From the Ashes*, p.21.

[107]Lawyers Committee interview, May 23, 1988.

September the Serrano investigation had widened, with ballistic testing linking the bullets to three other unsolved murders; in at least one of these killings, officials have in the past suggested the FMLN was responsible.

Reached by telephone in April 1989, Justice Minister Samayoa said the "investigation is still pending....It's difficult to say who killed Judge Serrano. In this country, it could be anybody."

A review of files in the Serrano case on April 3, 1989, revealed that the Attorney General's office petitioned the judge repeatedly to request information on the case from the SIU and the Security Forces. Only when it was presented for the third time was the petition granted.

In our view, the course of the Serrano case is yet another illustration of how, more often than not, investigations are colored more by the desire to score political points than to pursue justice honestly.

B. REVISORY COMMISSION ON SALVADORAN LEGISLATION

The Revisory Commission on Salvadoran Legislation, known as CORELESAL, was created by Legislative Decree No. 39 on June 13, 1985, and according to Article One of the decree has the following objectives:

> a) to conduct critical studies and analyses of the judicial system, and civil and penal laws, regulations, and procedures.

> b) after these studies, to elaborate laws and regulations which incorporate the proposed reforms; these projects should aim to adapt secondary laws to the Constitution and to improve the justice system.[108]

According to AID's Office of Democratic Initiatives, which administers the Administration of Justice Program, $853,438 had been spent on the Revisory Commission through June 30, 1988 and another $2.2 million had been obligated but not expended. A summary of the Judicial Reform Program provided to the Lawyers Committee in November 1988 shows AID had budgeted $2.6 million for CORELESAL; an additional $380,000 was contributed by the Salvadoran government in counterpart funds, for a project total exceeding $3 million.

According to Dr. Jose Ernesto Criollo, CORELESAL's Executive Secretary, the Commission employs 20 support staff and 20 attorneys, who are divided into three work areas: Penal, Civil, and Administrative.[109] Each team is responsible for conducting studies and proposing legal reform in its area of expertise. Draft legislation is sent out for discussion in the legal community and on several occasions public fora have been held to debate the proposals. Suggestions are then incorporated into the draft. Before submission

---

[108]Editorial, *CORELESAL-Informa*, June 1987, No.1., p. 3.

[109]Lawyers Committee interview with Dr. Jose Ernesto Criollo, CORELESAL offices, San Salvador, July 8, 1988.

to the Legislative Assembly for discussion and a vote, the proposal must be approved by the 10-member Commission.[110]

The work of the Penal team seeks to: guarantee the rights of defendants; reduce criminality and the incidence of crimes being committed with impunity; update criminal legislation; streamline the criminal process to ensure rapid investigation of crimes; and incorporate more efficient means of scientific evidence into criminal legislation.[111]

The Civil team's objectives include: conform civil legislation to the country's current situation; initiate basic research and formulate a legal framework that will lead to reforms in the family code; and simplify civil and commercial procedures to ensure prompt and complete justice.

The objectives of the third work area, covering administrative law and procedures, are to: formulate draft legislation for the National Council on the Judiciary and the Judicial Career; revise the law governing constitutional procedures; supervise studies and investigations of the administration of justice, the judicial branch, and the penitentiary system and to make recommendations; and prepare groundwork for a study of children and the law.

Article 271 of the 1983 Salvadoran Constitution says that all secondary legislation shall be brought into harmony with the new Constitution by December 20, 1984, that is, one year after it took effect. A number of discrepancies exist, and it could be argued that CORELESAL had a constitutional mandate to tackle these issues.

---

[110]CORELESAL consists of 10 members appointed by the President: 2 Supreme Court Magistrates; 1 representative of the Attorney General; 1 representative of the Solicitor General; 1 representative of the Ministry of Justice; 1 representative of the Ministry of Defense and Public Security; 2 representatives of the Bar Associations; 2 representatives of the Law Faculties; 1 representative of the President of the Republic, serving as Executive Secretary.

[111]"Proyecto de Reforma Judicial, Comision Revisora de la Legislacion Salvadorena," *CORELESAL-Informa*, June 1987, No.1, pp. 6-7.

Executive Secretary Dr. Jose Ernesto Criollo said his Commission was in fact "obligated to deal with" these discrepancies.[112]

Auxiliary Organs of the Court

One key issue that the Revisory Commission has thus far failed to address is Article 11 of the Criminal Procedure Code which designates the three Security Forces as "auxiliary organs for the administration of justice." Only officially designated auxiliary organs are authorized to collect evidence for use in judicial proceedings. In practice, this means that only evidence gathered by detectives of the National Police, Treasury Police, or National Guard is admissible in court, excluding material collected by, for example, the Human Rights Department of the Attorney General's office.

Given the human rights record of the Security Forces, the problems with this system are obvious. Because of Article 11's restrictions, SIU staff must be drawn from the three Security Forces, who owe their primary loyalty to the Armed Forces. Since policemen and soldiers are implicated in many of the most sensitive human rights cases, the effect of Article 11 is to require the military to investigate itself. The record is clear: El Salvador's Armed Forces are either unwilling or incapable of cleaning their own house.

Council on the Judiciary

One law drafted by the Commission that could have some impact is the proposal for a Council on the Judiciary allowing for the merit selection of First Instance judges and magistrates in Second Instance Chambers.[113] If and when this proposal is given

---

[112]Lawyers Committee interview with Dr. Jose Ernesto Criollo, CORELESAL offices, San Salvador, July 8, 1988.
Some of those areas of the law not in accord with the 1983 Constitution concern the death penalty, military draft, and the labor code. Given that ARENA now controls the Legislative Assembly, thoroughgoing reforms are unlikely.

[113]*Magistrados de Camaras de Segunda Instancia* and *Jueces de Primera Instancia*; Second Instance Courts are primarily intermediate appelate courts, except in San Salvador where they are charged with trying crimes "against the State." First Instance Courts are primary trial courts and also hear appeals from rulings of

serious consideration, it will be controversial. Under the current system, the Legislative Assembly appoints the Supreme Court for a five-year term.[114] The high court, in turn, makes appointments to all lower benches and auxiliary personnel. Under the proposal, judges will be chosen by a nine-member Council, consisting of representatives of the legal community.[115]

---

justices of the peace.

[114]Article 182, Paragraph 9 of the Constitution specifies that the Supreme Court shall "Name Magistrates to Second Instance Chambers, Judges of First Instance, and Justices of the Peace; forensic doctors and the Court personnel; remove them, receive their resignations, and grant leaves of absence."
Article 186 says "A Judicial Career is to be established"; Judges "should enjoy job stability." Article 187 names the National Council on the Judiciary as the body mandated to propose candidates for First and Second Instance judges.
Neither of these provisions has been implemented and the appointment of court personnel remains political from top to bottom. The political parties are apt to oppose any attempt to strip them of this right. In fact, in 1986 an informal agreement was made stipulating that the three main right-wing parties, ARENA, the PCN, and PAISA, would each appoint a third of the justices of the peace. In practice, this has not necessarily meant that the appointees are aligned with these three political parties. An AID-funded study of the Salvadoran Court System observed of the Justices of the Peace: "...due to their grassroots jurisdiction, it is unlikely that the political parties would be amenable to include them within a career judiciary."
"El Salvador Sector Assessment: Court Administration," Executive Summary, Center for the Administration of Justice, Florida International University, October 1987, p.8. The study was conducted jointly by FIU, ILANUD, and CORELESAL.

[115]The nine members are 3 magistrates of the Supreme Court; one Second Instance Magistrate; one First Instance Judge; an attorney from the Attorney General's office; an attorney from the Solicitor General's office; an attorney named by the Federation of Associations of Lawyers of El Salvador; an attorney named by the law faculties. Each institution is to choose its own representative. See Chapter 2, Article 5 and 6 of *Ley del Consejo Nacional de la Judicatora* (CORELESAL, June 1988).

The current Supreme Court was appointed by the ARENA-dominated Constituent Assembly in 1984 and the current ARENA-controlled Legislative Assembly may choose a new court when the term is up in June 1989, or opt to reappoint the bench. It is unlikely that the Right will legislate away its right to appoint the judiciary, which it has dominated since 1984. Yet an AID official -- reflecting views expressed at a forum on merit selection -- predicted passage of the proposal. "There's a consensus that merit selection is better. The issue is not so much to remove political decision-making, but to inject quality," he said.[116]

The Record

To date, seven proposed laws have been submitted by the Revisory Commission to the Legislative Assembly:

a) definition of the small farmer;

b) a reform of Decree 50, which regulates detention and processing procedures during a State of Exception;

c) reforms to the Criminal Procedure Code;

d) a law regulating the use of surnames;

e) a law creating a National Council of the Judiciary;

f) modification of the jury system; and

g) modification of the Criminal Procedure Code concerning the trial, or plenary phase of a case.

The Assembly approved the draft legislation defining the small farmer in late 1986. The remaining six proposals are still officially pending.

Submitted to the Assembly on February 23, 1987, CORELESAL's Law on Penal Procedure During States of Exception was based on an 819-page, two-volume study. The draft proposed significant reforms to the much-criticized Decree 50, enacted on February 24, 1984.

---

[116]Lawyers Committee interview, AID, San Salvador, May 23, 1988.

Yet in March 1987, CORELESAL's proposal was virtually ignored when the legislature enacted Decree 618, which was basically identical to Decree 50. "They didn't even consider our proposal," Dr. Criollo told the Lawyers Committee.

An AID official in San Salvador said that CORELESAL's substitute for Decree 50 was "very controversial. Perhaps it was too idealistic to be feasible."[117] Another Embassy official called the proposal "misguided...they didn't acknowledge what a military needs to fight a war. The task is, how to protect human rights given the military's power."[118]

Potentially Useful Studies

CORELESAL has seemingly been most active and effective in convening fora for discussion of issues facing the legal community.[119] By sending out draft laws for review by attorneys, judges, and law faculties, CORELESAL has conceivably served to raise the level of debate within the legal community.

Several potentially useful studies have also been produced under its auspices.[120] One such study on the prison population

---

[117]Lawyers Committee interview, AID, San Salvador, July 5, 1988.

[118]Lawyers Committee interview, U.S. Embassy, May 25, 1988.

[119]Among these conferences was a March 1987 symposium on the National Council on the Judiciary and Judicial Careers. In December 1987, two seminars were held in conjunction with the Salvadoran Supreme Court and the American Bar Association addressing arbitration in commercial and labor law. In February 1988, a meeting was convened in San Miguel to discuss a proposed code of ethics for the legal profession. CORELESAL also sponsored a symposium on the regulation of the use of names, thereafter publishing a list of "curious" names given to babies logged at San Salvador's birth registry. See *CORELESAL-Informa*, June 1987, No. 1, p.17.

[120]CORELESAL participated in a major assessment of the Salvadoran court system conducted jointly with the United Nations Latin American Institute for the Prevention of Crime and Treatment

revealed that over 92% of the country's inmates were in pretrial detention; 34% of the cases were still in the preliminary investigatory phase (*fase de instruccion*). Further, 5% of the 5,381 prisoners held in July 1987 had already completed the maximum sentence possible had their cases been tried. The Commission's study built on work done by a UN agency, which found that El Salvador placed third after Bolivia and Paraguay in the numbers of unsentenced detainees.[121]

CORELESAL defines itself as a "nationally projected program which goes beyond the interests of party politics and the particular interests of the institutions represented on the Commission, to convert itself into a patriotic and civic interest group." The Commission says it "seeks Salvadoran solutions to the nation's problems...."[122] In our interview, Dr. Criollo expressed a similar goal, saying that "Our work is not politicized. We think of things at a higher, structural level."

For the most part, the Commission has yet to tackle some of the country's most obvious needs, such as a military service law and reform of the labor code.[123] Dr. Criollo told the Lawyers

---

of Offenders (ILANUD) and the Center for Administration of Justice at Florida International University. Their 170-page report was issued on September 28, 1987 as *Diagnostico Sobre el Organo Judicial en El Salvador*.

The report appears to be a thorough assessment of the problems and shortcomings of the judicial system, viewed largely in technical terms. One factor notably absent in the analysis is the nearly 10-year-old civil war, which is universally considered to have made a poor system a lot worse. The study recommends, for example, that "justices of the peace be required to reside in the area in which they serve," seemingly unaware of the fact that many justices have left the areas of heaviest combat. Others have been threatened into leaving by the FMLN.

[121]See *Diario de Hoy*, April 26, 1988; *CORELESAL-Informa*, December 1987, no.3, pp. 8-10.

[122]*CORELESAL-Informa*, June 1987, no. 1, pp. 7-8.

[123]For a discussion of the Labor Code's shortcomings and an analysis of two reform proposals, see *Labor Rights in El Salvador* (Americas Watch, March 1988), Chapter V, "The Prospects for Reform," pp.91-95. To take one example, the Constitution gives

Committee that CORELESAL did not plan to prepare a military service law "since we have enough to do" and offered that the Ministry of Defense was drafting one. [124]

Another matter in need of CORELESAL attention is the Commission on Investigations, whose authorization ran out in July 1987. By that date CORELESAL was to have made a recommendation how to institutionalize the Commission on Investigations. The date passed with no comment. "For various political reasons, they decided not to make a decision," an AID official told the Lawyers Committee.[125]

Despite the fact that CORELESAL appears well funded and well staffed by competent professionals, studies and proposals seem to progress at a snail's pace.[126] The Commission's newsletter describes numerous works in progress, yet only seven proposals have been drafted into legislation and presented to the Assembly.[127] AID target dates for completion of work are regularly not met; one

---

farmworkers the right to organize -- a right not recognized, and hence not granted, in the Labor Code.

[124]Lawyers Committee interview with Dr. Criollo, July 8, 1988.

[125]Lawyers Committee interview, AID, San Salvador, May 23, 1988.

[126]The outside evaluating team found CORELESAL to be staffed by "outstanding professionals.[...]This is due in large part to the salary levels set by the Commission." Mudge, et al., March 1988, p. 30.

On the negative side, we heard grumblings of resentment from other attorneys and judges who complained about the high salaries of Commission staff which, in their view, were unwarranted given CORELESAL's meager output.

[127]Among the works in progress are reforms to the jury system; proposals on constitutional procedures; assessment of fines; recommendations on unsentenced prisoners; a proposal on notaries; streamlining case management; draft law on adoptions; reform of law on commercial procedure and arbitration; and a diagnostic study of the penitentiary system and rehabilitation. Responding to criticism, Commission staff agreed to delay new projects until some work in progress is completed, according to an AID Semiannual Project Status Report for October 1987 - March 1988.

example is the new adoption law, which was to be ready by September 1988.

One problem recognized by AID is that once draft legislation makes it to the Assembly it tends to sit because no legislator feels ownership of the project. "If a proposal didn't have a godfather in the Assembly, it didn't move," an AID official told the Lawyers Committee.[128]   Nominally the proposals are submitted by the Minister of Justice, whose representative sits on the Commission. "Yet he plays no active role. And now it would be the kiss of death for the Christian Democrats to submit something," the official observed, in light of the fact that the ARENA party has dominated the legislature since March 1988.[129]

CORELESAL has now been encouraged to develop strategies for getting the legislature to act. Dr. Criollo told the Lawyers Committee last July that he planned to meet with the heads of each faction in the Assembly to brief them on CORELESAL's program and the draft legislation to be presented. "We have little power," he said, "and no party lines."[130]

---

[128]Lawyers Committee interview, AID, July 5, 1988.

[129]The Project Status Report for the Judicial Reform Project provided to the Lawyers Committee in February 1989 addresses the problems in getting proposals through the Assembly: "Problems have been encountered at the stage of approval of each draft by the legislature. The main problem appears to be a lack of interest and time from the members of the legislature who have been focussing their attention on last year's elections and on more politically oriented affairs." p.90.

[130]Lawyers Committee interview with Dr. Jose Ernesto Criollo, July 8, 1988.
The evaluating team observed that CORELESAL, "constituted largely of representatives of the judiciary [dominated by the Right] did not enjoy the closest of working relationships with the Executive Branch [dominated by the PDC]." The evaluators found it appropriate that the government, with its three Commission members, take primary responsibility for shepherding draft legislation through the process. Mudge, March 1988, pp.8 and 32.

Minimal Progress

A U.S. Embassy statement in January 1988 reported that CORELESAL's "[p]rogress has been considerable."[131] In San Salvador, an AID official told the Lawyers Committee in May that "Results are very encouraging and positive."[132] Yet measured against their own objectives as described above -- which were published in the Commission's newsletter two years after work had begun -- the Lawyers Committee concludes that the Commission's progress has in fact been minimal. The lack of progress is especially apparent in those critical areas which could have a favorable impact on the administration of justice and improve the country's human rights record. Closer to the truth is the assessment of a State Department official who told the Lawyers Committee in April 1988 that CORELESAL's work had yielded "nothing earth-shattering. [...] It's really hard to say what the results are for the Revisory Commission," the official concluded.

While the Lawyers Committee recogizes the need for a new institution to establish its credentials before throwing itself into the fray, the Revisory Commission's performance to date suggests little reason for optimism that it will even address key issues affecting the Salvadoran legal system. After more than three and a half years, the Revisory Commission is no longer in infancy. In fact, attempts at judicial reform go back six years to the presidency of Alvaro Magana.[133] In practice, no such institution functions in a political

---

[131]"El Salvador: Judicial Reform Program," July 15, 1987, updated January 19, 1988, p.2.

[132]Lawyers Committee interview, AID, May 23, 1988.

[133]Provisional President Magana initiated negotiations with AID in 1983 which resulted in the original $3 million grant for judicial reform. The first revisory commission and the training of guards for the Churchwomen's trial in 1984 were its first two projects. CORELESAL's precursor was known as the Revisory Commission for the Administration of Justice in Penal and Civil Matters created by Executive Agreement 145 of November 11, 1984. According to a study published by the International Human Rights Law Group, the only product of this first U.S.-funded commission was Decree 50, the state of emergency legislation which lapsed on its own terms in January 1987. See *Waiting for Justice: Treatment of Political Prisoners Under El Salvador's Decree 50* (IHRLG, Washington, D.C.,

65

vacuum, particularly in El Salvador's current climate. A civil war has raged for nearly 10 years and 70,000 lives have been lost. Egregious human rights violations have been committed, and continue today at an alarming rate. The bulk of these violations are still committed by uniformed members of the country's Armed Forces.

Given these realities, there is little evidence that the work of CORELESAL has made a serious contribution to correcting the near paralysis in which the country's justice system finds itself, or to addressing the institutional and legal obstacles to ensuring respect for fundamental human rights.

March 1987) p.10.

C. JUDICIAL PROTECTION UNIT

The Judicial Protection Unit (JPU) was created to help protect participants in controversial human rights cases, including judges, lawyers, jurors and witnesses. The initial impetus for the unit was concern about the safety of participants in the prosecution of five National Guardsmen who were tried in May 1984 for killing four U.S. churchwomen. Several months prior to that trial, a unit of 60 guards from Mariona Prison were given a one-week course -- which "focussed heavily on firearms training"[134] -- at the Federal Law Enforcement Training Center (FLETC) at Glynco, Georgia. Trained by the U.S. Marshall Service, the men were then deployed to provide protection on the day of the trial. "It was bare-bones training," an AID official involved in the program recalls. "We put it together in three to four weeks. They weren't given any uniforms or equipment. The whole thing was unfortunate."[135]

In 1987 the Lawyers Committee noted that at the trial of the churchwomen's case, the "performance of the unit was hardly distinguished. The trial was hours old and an undisciplined crowd of hundreds of reporters and others had already packed the courthouse and the surrounding streets before the unit even arrived at the scene.

"The caliber of the unit's members was widely criticized. As one high-ranking government official told [the Lawyers Committee]:

a good Judicial Protection Unit would need members (1) who are not poorly educated, (2) who are not already practiced in the past abuses of the security forces, and (3) who are not psychopaths. Unfortunately, most of the original 60 failed one of those tests and some failed all three.[136]

---

[134]Mudge, *et al*, p. 21.

[135]Lawyers Committee telephone interview with an AID official in Washington, D.C., February 15, 1989.

[136]Lawyers Committee interview, San Salvador, October 16, 1985.

Another suggested to us that the use of prison guards to make up the unit was part of the problem. Prison guards, he said, are men who could not make it in the Salvadoran Armed Forces."[137]

The unit was disbanded after the trial, and has since only been used once, in the February 1986 trial of two gunmen accused of murdering a Salvadoran land reform official and two U.S. labor advisors in 1981.[138]

Nonetheless, the JPU was given official imprimatur by Decree No. 66 on September 25, 1985.[139] The Judicial Reform Program includes $1.2 million for the JPU, plus $900,000 in counterpart funds from the Salvadoran government for a total of $2.1 million. According to AID, $310,000 has been spent on the JPU and another $400,000 obligated. The bulk of the funds are in escrow, awaiting the outcome of discussions about the unit's future.

An Assessment

Both U.S. officials and outside observers have criticized the JPU. A State Department official told the Lawyers Committee that the project was "ill conceived from the beginning."[140] An AID official in San Salvador called the project "rather stillborn."[141] The outside evaluating team hired by AID called it the "one real design 'dud'...

representing a rushed effort to adapt a relatively

---

[137]*From the Ashes*, p.37.

[138]According to an official in AID's Office of Democratic Initiatives at the U.S. Embassy, a few of the men also provided protection to those implicated in the Armenia well killings. Lawyers Committee phone interview, March 15, 1989. Yet as a discrete unit, the JPU ceased to exist after the churchwomen's trial.

[139]According to the evaluating team, the Ministry of Justice issued a plan of action in March 1986, whereby the JPU -- staffed by penitentiary guards -- would report directly to the ministry. See Mudge, *et al.*, p. 25.

[140]Lawyers Committee interview at the State Department, April 6, 1988.

[141]Lawyers Committee interview, AID, May 23, 1988.

foreign concept with insufficient Salvadoran input. Indeed, the establishment of the guard force for the trial of the Nuns' case was viewed by the Salvadorans as primarily a U.S. Government operation. Salvadoran participation was limited to provision of the guards, and hardly elite guards at that. [142]

While nobody defends the record, identifying lessons that can be drawn from the 1984 experience and agreeing on a future model for the unit has proved difficult. The AID evaluating team wrote:

> the experience gained is difficult to reconstruct three years later.... It appears, however, that the protection provided by the JPU at that time was purely a display of armed guards for the occasion, with little consideration given to long range planning for future contingencies. This effort did not accomplish much in instilling public confidence in the integrity or safety of the judicial system.[143]

The Future of the Judicial Protection Unit

Since the JPU was formed in 1984, a variety of differing conceptions have been proposed by U.S. and Salvadoran officials, with several different Salvadoran institutions seeking to assume control of the unit.

There have been several different proposals concerning where the JPU should be based, among them the Supreme Court,[144] the Attorney General's office, the Ministry of Justice, and the Commission on Investigations. A military officer interviewed by

---

[142]Mudge, *et al.* p.40.

[143]Mudge, *et al.* p.20.

[144]In an interview with the Lawyers Committee on January 11, 1989, the new Attorney General -- imposed by the ARENA-dominated Assembly -- belittled Supreme Court President Guerrero's scheme for a unit under his control that would protect all trial participants. "It's a romantic notion," said Roberto Garcia Alvarado. "That takes money and this country is bankrupt!"

the AID evaluating team argued that it should be organized by the National Police and National Guard.[145]

U.S. officials have suggested forming a risk assessment team, a small group trained to assess danger and need in a given case. Outside contractors would provide protection if deemed necessary. The external evaluation team suggested that protection could be provided by the Security Forces, "or private contractors as needed and appropriate...."[146]

While favoring eventual civilian control, the evaluators recommended that the JPU be placed on an interim basis under the jurisdiction of the Commission on Investigations' Executive Unit, which is headed by two colonels.[147] They made this recommendation "because of the need for firm, effective management and direction on a professional level and for close coordination and cooperation with the SIU."[148] Inexplicably, the study found that "Placing the JPU under another organization would risk increased military control or politicizing the function. There might be a tendency to use JPU resources for parochial priorities."

We believe that placing the unit under the Commission on Investigations would only exacerbate existing problems. Despite official protestations to the contrary, there is little evidence that the Commission's forensic and investigatory activities are actually under civilian authority. In practice, there would be no meaningful distinction between placing the JPU at the Commission and placing it directly under one of the three Security Forces.

The suggestion that the JPU be housed at the Special Investigative Unit -- under the control of military officers -- has apparently caused some discussion and disquiet among Embassy staff. One AID official told the Lawyers Committee, "There's a

---

[145]Mudge, et al., p. 22.

[146]Mudge, et al., p.23.

[147]The team found that the "Judicial Protection Unit should logically be with the judicial branch...." Mudge, et al., p.50.

[148]Mudge et al., p.24.

hesitancy to finance a police force, or to place the unit under two military officers at the Executive Unit." [149]

The Embassy's solution was to make the unit answerable to the Commission on Investigations, headed by Justice Minister Julio Samayoa. AID's most recent Project Status Report says that President Duarte and SETEFE (the government planning bureau) have agreed to the "new concept of a small risk assessment team to be located under the Commission on Investigations." Discussions were held with the Security Forces, but apparently AID does not consider the decision final, observing that there is lack of support for the notion from "key [Salvadoran government] players" as well as unnamed "legal impediments."

While the JPU was ill-conceived from the beginning, we have no doubt that there continues to be an acute need for protection in politically sensitive cases. Over our months of research in El Salvador, we have heard numerous accounts from judges, attorneys, and witnesses who regularly receive harassing phone calls and visits, often threatened with violence and even death.

The war and an antiquated and underfunded justice system serve to impede the prosecution of cases, especially sensitive ones. But if case participants fear that actively pursuing justice may lead to their own death, there is little hope for more accountability for those who violate fundamental human rights. The murder of Judge Jorge Alberto Serrano Panameno in May 1988 underlines the need for better means of protection for judges, jurors, and others involved in sensitive cases.

No amount of guard training or weaponry, however, will provide adequate security. Fundamental to a secure environment in which cases may proceed unimpeded is a commitment to an impartial justice system, free from fear and pressure by those who would use the system to their own ends and ensure impunity for even the most outrageous of criminal acts. Until the climate of fear and violence fostered by the war ends and changes are made by those Salvadorans who thwart justice -- and those U.S. officials who explain away their crimes -- any conceivable JPU model can only be minimally successful.

---

[149]Lawyers Committee interview, September 1988.

D. JUDICIAL ADMINISTRATION AND TRAINING

The fourth component of El Salvador's Judicial Reform Program is designed to "improve the Court system's administrative management, human resources, and physical facilities."[150] Some $3.5 million[151] has been allocated for supplies and training for judges, justices of the peace, and other court personnel. Since this program attempts to remedy technical deficiencies in the justice system and the lack of training by practitioners, it is perhaps the component most likely to fulfill its own objectives. These objectives, however, are insignificant given the near collapse of the judicial system. Money granted to buy filing cabinets, build temporary tribunals,[152] or publish a one volume compilation of the most common laws, to name a few projects, can at best improve the system's efficiency. Moreover, given the differences in U.S. and Salvadoran justice systems, the United States is perhaps the least appropriate donor for this kind of aid. El Salvador's legal system is based on the Napoleonic Code,[153] while the U.S. is based on English Common Law. Only the state of Louisiana has a similar system.

Compounding the problem is the enormous U.S. involvement in El Salvador since 1980, including over $3 billion in aid. We found some lawyers and judges resentful of U.S. "meddling" in yet another aspect of Salvadoran life. "They are imposing U.S. solutions

---

[150]"El Salvador, Judicial Reform Program," AID, March 17, 1988.

[151]Roughly half of the $3.5 million was donated by AID; the rest is the Salvadoran government's contribution, which actually stems from local currency generated by U.S. Economic Support Funds.

[152]San Salvador's main court building was damaged during the October 1986 earthquake. The tribunals functioned outside under tin roofs until August 1988, when temporary buildings were ready for occupation. The buildings were paid for out of reprogrammed earthquake relief funds from the United States.

[153]This system is also referred to as Civil Law. An AID official in San Salvador said that while the differences between the two systems are not an obstacle to the program, "We are careful not to impose our approach on them." Lawyers Committee interview, U.S. Embassy, July 5, 1988.

to Salvadoran problems," one conservative criminal judge told us, commenting on the AID program.

The Program

Component four funding has been used to buy equipment such as bicycles, motorbikes, and other vehicles; typewriters; tape recorders; and filing cabinets. A procedural manual for Justices of the Peace has been updated and printed and the Judicial Gazette is publishing again after a 10-year interruption. But the centerpiece of this part of the reform program is the training of judges, Justices of the Peace, and other court employees. According to AID, some 653 judicial personnel have received training.

Courses have been offered within El Salvador by U.S. consultants contracted by AID and by the staff of the United Nations Latin American Institute for the Prevention of Crime and the Treatment of Offenders (ILANUD), a now largely AID-funded institution based in San Jose, Costa Rica. A training unit has been formed within the Supreme Court, which will eventually assume training responsibilities, employing curriculum developed by ILANUD.

In 1987 nearly all the country's Justices of the Peace went through a rudimentary training course and follow-up seminars were offered in summer 1988. Many justices have no legal training and given the justice system's poor resources, do not even have a basic law library on hand.[154]

---

[154]Article 43 of the Law of the Judicial Branch establishes the following requirements for Justices of the Peace:
1. Salvadoran citizen.
2. In the capital, departmental capitals, and other cities the Supreme Court deems convenient, the office may only be held by lawyers or law students. In the rest of the country it is only necessary to have a notion of the law.
3. Over 21 years of age.
4. Having exercised political rights three years prior to appointment.
5. Named by the Supreme Court.
6. Two year term of office.
7. Of known morality and competency.
Incompatibilities:
1. Not blind or deaf.

Some 60 Salvadorans have also attended workshops abroad. Supreme Court President Francisco Jose Guerrero told the Lawyers Committee that 50 Justices of the Peace "were sent to Louisiana to learn what a judge is in the United States and learn what dignity a judge has."[155] High-ranking court personnel have been sent on study tours to the United States,[156] and one penal judge attended a training seminar in Spain, at AID's expense.

The team contracted by AID to evaluate the judicial reform program observed that while training "must be extended and made a regular part of the system" [...] we are skeptical that training in the United States or other foreign locations is cost effective, but it may be desirable on a modest scale."[157] The team recommended increased reliance on ILANUD and other countries of the Civil Law tradition such as Spain, Italy, and France.[158] The President of the

---

2. No drunks, gamblers, or drug addicts.
3. No clergy permitted.
Justices of the Peace are the first line of defense in the Salvadoran system, handling the most basic day-to-day criminal or legal matters at the community level.

[155]Lawyers Committee interview, Supreme Court, September 14, 1988.

[156]Some training has been done in cooperation with the American Bar Association and the law school of Louisiana State University, according to AID's Office of Democratic Initiatives in San Salvador. An ABA associate told the Lawyers Committee in March 1989 that they have received some $60,000 over the last two years from AID for training in El Salvador, which has included seminars in commercial and labor arbitration; judicial review; and how to administer a court room.

[157]Mudge, et. al., pp.38-39.

[158]"For AID we suggest the importance of determining division of labor with other donors, particularly civil law countries in a better position to help the Salvadoran legal system with the substance of legal and systemic reform. Secondly, the AID Mission needs to pursue further the utility of regional programs to supplement the current bilateral project in addressing the specific needs of Salvadoran judicial reform." Mudge, et. al., p.5.

Supreme Court, Francisco Jose Guerrero, told the Lawyers Committee that he aimed to expand existing cooperation with Spain.

Under AID and ILANUD's tutelage, law libraries have been established in San Salvador, Santa Ana, and San Miguel which Guerrero said he found "more elaborate than we needed, perhaps."[159] He said he sought funding for travelling libraries -- an air-conditioned bus with a xerox machine -- that could visit a remote community for three to four days, providing local court practitioners with access to legal materials.

One plan which has been delayed is the establishment of five model courts in the penal, civil, traffic, and housing sectors. Groundwork has now been laid by the Revisory Commission, and the project is slated for mid-1989. An AID official told the Lawyers Committee they had originally planned to choose existing tribunals, making them into "demonstration courts" by giving them all the "good equipment, focussing our training there, having them implement good court procedures."[160] One setback to the program was a failure to obtain overtime funding from the Supreme Court for full-time personnel. Until March 1989, the courts only worked a 30-hour week, now raised to 37 hours in San Salvador, a normal work week for the Salvadoran government.

AID now says that the "model courts" will likely not be identified among exisiting ones, but fabricated from ground up. In our view, this decision is misguided, indicating another step toward creating parallel structures alongside existing institutions in the justice system. Demonstration courts can only yield demonstration justice.

We agree with the AID official who conceded, "Just buying filing cabinets, what good does it really do? You can't get too far ahead of a government."[161] Even the best and most-needed technical improvements in the system will not cause meaningful change in El Salvador's human rights record as long as there is no commitment to enforce existing laws and hold violators accountable.

---

[159]Lawyers Committee interview, Supreme Court, September 14, 1988, San Salvador.

[160]Lawyers Committee interview, U.S. Embassy, October 4, 1988.

[161]Lawyers Committee interview, U.S. Embassy, July 5, 1988.

"If you can threaten a judge by telling him, 'I'm going to kill you,' what difference does it make what the Penal Code says?" the AID official continued. "What difference does it make what the code on penal procedure says if the police don't follow it?"

CHAPTER III: ESCALATING VIOLENCE (1987-1989)

A. RECENT POLITICAL ATTACKS

Despite international pressure and efforts to curb political violence through programs such as the Administration of Justice, the violence continues. In fact, there has been a considerable increase in political violence in the last year. Though the level of killings has declined considerably since the early 1980's, the current monthly toll, including some death squad-style murders, is a disturbing indicator of the continuing erosion of respect for human rights in El Salvador.

According to Tutela Legal, the human rights office of the Catholic Archdiocese of San Salvador, in 1988 Salvadoran government forces were responsible for 92 killings of non-combatant civilians; 112 people whom witnesses observed being detained have never been located; 46 disappeared altogether. During the same period Tutela Legal lists 44 cases of political killings of non-combatants by the Farabundo Marti Front for National Liberation (FMLN).

Right-wing death squads assassinated 60 Salvadorans last year, according to archdiocesan monitors. In the early 1980's when the death squads unleashed a reign of terror, their integral links to the Salvadoran military were well documented. In April 1988, the State Department reported to the Congress that:

It is generally acknowledged that deaths squads of the right -- often comprised of active duty military or security force personnel operating with the complicity of some senior officers of the armed forces -- were responsible for thousands of murders.[162]

In his 1989 report to the United Nations Commission on Human Rights, Professor Jose Antonio Pastor Ridruejo, the Special Representative on El Salvador, described the current upsurge in violence in the following way:

An alarming number of politically motivated summary executions, including mass executions, have been carried out by members of the State apparatus, particularly members of the Armed Forces, to the

---

[162]"Report on the Situation in El Salvador," April 1, 1988, p.22.

point that the clear downward trend in such crimes that occurred after Mr. Duarte took office as Constitutional President of the Republic has been reversed.[163]

Despite public statements to the contrary, the Armed Forces still fiercely resist investigations into recent political killings and other violence. Their obstinacy extends even to cases where ample evidence has been collected by rights monitors and Church groups. What has changed is the sophistication of their cover-up and the accompanying publicity campaign.

In the following section we summarize eight recent cases of political killing or attempted killing. In each of these cases, information compiled by nongovernmental organizations suggests that the Salvadoran military, Security Forces, or Civil Defense are implicated. In each of these cases we summarize the limited steps that have been taken to initiate investigations. Unfortunately, our review of these and other recent cases leads us to conclude that members of El Salvador's Armed Forces -- triggermen as well as those who order them to kill -- continue to be virtually immune from successful prosecution.

---

[163] "Informe definitivo a la Comision de Derechos Humanos sobre la situacion de los derechos humanos en El Salvador que presenta el Sr. Jose Antonio Pastor Ridruejo, en cuplimiento del mandato conferido por la resolucion 1988/65 de dicha Comision," E/CN.4/1989/23, (February 2, 1989) paragraph 96, p. 22.

San Francisco Massacre
September 21, 1988

The Detention and Killings

A few hours after darkness on September 20, 1988, some 100 soldiers of the Jiboa Battalion of the Fifth Infantry Brigade marched into the small village of San Francisco, jurisdiction of San Sebastian in the Department of San Vicente. San Francisco, abandoned years ago because of aerial bombardment, was repopulated in 1986. Around 10:00 p.m., the military men took Jose Maria Flores, 40, from his home; by noon the following day soldiers had searched the homes of most of the village's 15 families, detaining nearly 50 persons. Some were intercepted en route to jobs, school, or chores along San Francisco's dirt paths.[164]

Some 40 of the the town's men, women, and children were held under guard by two dozen soldiers in an abandoned schoolhouse. Flores was forced into the adjacent communal outhouses along with five other men: Jesus Zepeda Rivas, 65; Jose Atilio Rivas, 50; Jose Nicolas Flores Alfaro, 27; Jose Ulises Sibrian Rivas, 40; and Francisco Alfaro, 50. In the schoolhouse soldiers accused their captives of collaborating with the guerrillas. Several inhabitants who had been captured at 6 a.m. said that the soldiers provided neither food nor water during the 12-hour imprisonment in the school's cramped quarters.[165]

Soldiers reading from a list of names began to take individuals from the schoolhouse at 12:30 p.m. Over the next two hours they removed four women and one man, blindfolding them and binding their hands before questioning them. One woman taken outside, Rosa Emilia Rivas, was blindfolded, interrogated and later released when soldiers determined that she was not among those sought. She was permitted to return to the schoolhouse.[166]

---

[164]A Lawyers Committee representative interviewed witnessess at the site on September 22 and again on September 26, 1988.

[165]*Ibid.*

[166]Lawyers Committee interview with witnesses, September 22 and 26, 1988.

79

The other four -- Maria Zoila Rivas Sibrian, 48; Teresa de Jesus Argueta, 46; Maria de Jesus Sibrian, 27; and Francisco Alfaro, 50 -- and the six men who were taken from the outhouses, were led down a narrow dirt path where they were killed by high-powered firearms.

Witnesses who watched through a gap in the doorway as the ten were blindfolded and their hands bound said that at 3:30 p.m., about 20 minutes after the soldiers took their ten captives away, they heard two detonations followed by a round of gunfire. Several reported that a soldier who later returned to the schoolhouse remarked that some of the children would never see their parents again. Among those present in the schoolhouse was Juan Antonio Rivas, the teenage son of victim Maria Zoila Rivas, who had become worried when his mother failed to return from fetching water at the nearby stream. He was captured by soldiers as he searched for her, and taken to the school where his mother was also held. He later watched the soldiers take her away.[167]

An elderly woman was still outside her home when the soldiers went by with their captives. "Go inside. It's dangerous out here," instructed one of the soldiers. A short time later, she heard explosions and then a lot of shooting.[168]

The soldiers held the townspeople in the school until darkness, around 6 p.m. As they released them, the soldiers warned the people not to go down the road they led the others "because it was dangerous." None of the villagers ventured that way until the next morning, when the son of one of the victims found his father and the nine others dead. Found at the scene were piles of bloodstained leaflets and a large banner -- left by the FMLN, according to an Armed Forces press release.[169]

---

[167]Testimony of Juan Antonio Rivas taken by the non-governmental Human Rights Commission of El Salvador, September 26, 1988; also based on the testimony of a San Francisco resident taken by a Lawyers Committee representative, September 26, 1988.

[168]Testimony of a San Francisco resident, recorded by a Lawyers Committee repesentative on September 22, 1988.

[169]COPREFA Bulletin 272, September 23, 1988.

The Aftermath

By about the time that the bodies had been discovered, the Armed Forces press office issued a statement reporting that members of the Jiboa Battalion had surprised a guerrilla column near San Francisco, killing "ten subversives" in battle.[170] The following day, after the villagers had been interviewed by journalists and human rights monitors, the military issued a second version, now alleging that the soldiers had captured eight persons suspected of collaborating with the guerrillas, and were ambushed by rebels as they led their prisoners along the road toward a helicopter landing site in a neighboring village some two kilometers from San Francisco to the north. As a result of the combat, the statement said, all eight prisoners and two guerrillas were killed. An unidentified soldier was reportedly wounded.

The following day, President Duarte told reporters that "[o]bviously, if in that area [of San Francisco] there are people aligned with the Marxist sector the family members could lie...."[171] Duarte lamented that some "wish to convert all acts of combat into human rights cases," in order to embarrass the government during the upcoming visit of the United Nations Special Representative on Human Rights.[172] Referring to Army soldiers killed in Morazan days earlier, Duarte questioned why such persons didn't allege that the dead were actually peasants killed by guerrillas.[173] However, he added, the military and the Attorney General's office would mount separate investigations.

Soon after the killings, most of the village's inhabitants left for neighboring towns. When its investigators arrived in San

---

[170] COPREFA Bulletin 271, September 22, 1988.

[171]*The Miami Herald*, September 24, 1988.

[172]Professor Jose Antonio Pastor Ridruejo of Spain has been examining human rights in El Salvador since 1981 as the Special Representative of the Commission on Human Rights of the United Nations. In preparation for his 1989 report, Professor Pastor Ridruejo visited El Salvador from October 9-15, 1988.

[173]*El Mundo*, September 23, 1988. When a reporter pointed out that the San Francisco victims were chosen from a list of names, President Duarte said he was not aware of that fact, and requested more information.

Francisco to find the village mostly deserted, the Attorney General's office accused Tutela Legal, the Catholic Archdiocese's human rights office, and the nongovernmental Human Rights Commission (CDHES) of sabotaging their investigation by arriving with 15 trucks and taking the witnesses away.[174]

The Exhumation

In response to a formal request by the Attorney General's office, the judge of the First Instance from San Sebastian, Dr. Rafael Pena Marin, ordered seven bodies exhumed from two multiple graves behind the village church. These bodies, and two others buried in the municipal cemetery in San Sebastian, were exhumed on October 5. (The body of Francisco Alfaro, buried in a neighboring town, was not examined.) At the same time, the judge requested that the commander of the Fifth Brigade provide a list of names and other information on those who participated in the operation.

Despite requests by the Attorney General and the judge, the Commission on Investigations did not send personnel from its forensic unit to assist in the exhumation. A government official said that it had been impossible to meet the unit's security requirements, and that the advanced date (the exhumation had initially been set for October 14) allowed insufficient lead time to arrange its participation. The autopsies were therefore conducted by doctors attached to courts in San Salvador and San Sebastian. Human rights workers and journalists who traveled to the site watched as local peasants recruited by the court -- fortifying themselves along the way with alcohol -- dug up the graves and lifted the bodies from the earth.[175]

As the judge and investigators assembled with human rights monitors at San Sebastian, trucks of soldiers entered the town and continued along the road to the village of San Francisco. When exhumation observers made their way up the same road a half hour later, they encountered numerous leaflets, allegedly placed by the FMLN.

---

[174]Lawyers Committee interview with Lic. Arturo Lazo, Attorney General's office, September 27, 1988.

[175]Representatives of the Lawyers Committee and Americas Watch witnessed the exhumation on October 5, 1988.

Throughout the exhumation, soldiers from the Jiboa Battalion maintained a presence near the grave site and along the path where the bodies had been found. While the exhumation was still in progress, other supposedly FMLN leaflets were found strewn along this path by investigators examining the site of the killings. After the first seven bodies were exhumed, those present drove back along the road toward San Sebastian, finding still more leaflets signed by the FMLN which had not been present earlier that day.

Also found at the spot where the bodies had been discovered was a bloodstained shirt, tied into a circle as if for a blindfold, with pieces of bone sticking to it.

The forensic doctors reported that eight of the nine bodies examined displayed gunshot wounds in the head. Seven of the nine had visible powder burns, from which the doctors concluded that these victims had been shot from a distance of approximately 10-15 centimeters. Attorney General Roberto Giron Flores, citing the forensic doctors, said their findings eliminated the possibility that the victims had died in a shootout.[176]

Human rights monitors from Tutela Legal -- present at the exhumation -- agreed with the Attorney General's view of the forensic evidence, and accused the Army of executing all ten persons.[177] U.S. government officials expressed deep skepticism about the Army's versions of the events, and reported that a second military investigation had been commissioned to do a more thorough job. The U.S.-funded Commission on Investigations failed to act, according to U.S. Embassy sources, because President Duarte, who they said determines that Commission's docket, never instructed it to initiate an investigation.[178]

---

[176] *Diario Latino*, October 11, 1988.

[177] *El Mundo*, October 12, 1988; Tutela Legal Weekly Report, September 16-22, 1988, pp.16-17.

[178] Interview at the U.S. Embassy, October 6, 1988. According to the law creating the Commission on Investigations and its Special Investigative Unit, the Commission itself is mandated to launch investigations. Neither the law nor subsequent enabling legislation requires the President to initiate or request an investigation. In late March the Lawyers Committee was told that President Duarte and Defense Minister Vides Casanova have an informal agreement under which the SIU may not examine cases in which the Armed Forces

The chief of the Armed Forces at the time, Gen. Adolfo Onecifero Blandon, responded to the Attorney General's conclusions, saying he would await the report of the military's own investigation.[179] The Commander of the Fifth Brigade, Colonel Jose Emilio Chavez Caceres, continued to maintain that his investigation confirmed that the peasants had died in a guerrilla ambush.[180]

The Army's Third Version of Events

On October 29, Col. Chavez Caceres called a press conference at which he announced that the Army had proof that after the battle with soldiers, guerrillas had returned to the scene, firing on the ·corpses from close range in order to cast suspicion on the Army. He showed a videotape of three bodies as they were being lifted from the graves at the exhumation juxtaposed with footage of the same bodies taken, he said, just after the firefight with the guerrillas. According to Caceres, the Army's video proved that some of the wounds discovered during the October 5 autopsies were not initially present.[181] However, the two videos displayed opposite sides of the bodies, making it impossible to directly compare the wounded areas.[182] Col. Chavez Caceres did not explain why no witnesses recalled hearing a second round of gunfire that would have corresponded to the post-mortem attempts at mutilation.[183]

---

are implicated unless ordered to do so by Duarte, presumably after consultation with the Defense Minister. See *Ley de Creacion de la Comision de Investigacion de Hechos Delictivos.* For a discussion of the Commission, see page 41.

[179]*Diario Latino*, October 11, 1988.

[180]*El Mundo*, October 14, 1988. Gen. Blandon told one group of visiting U.S. attorneys that the military had concluded that the victims died in an ambush. [Meeting with delegation of U.S. attorneys, October 13, 1988.]

[181] Interview with a journalist present at the press conference, October 29, 1988.

[182]A Lawyers Committtee representative viewed the uncut version of the videotape at the U.S. Embassy, November 2, 1988.

[183] Interview with journalists present at the press conference, October 31, 1988.

Footage taken by the military on the day of the incident revealed another disturbing discrepancy in its third version of the events: one of the victims was shown lying on *top* of the large banner, which, according to the logic of the Army's explanation, (a) would have to have been placed by rebels when they returned to mutilate the bodies some time *after* the military's video was made; (b) was already on the road as the guerrillas lay in wait to ambush the soldiers and their prisoners; or (c) was placed under the man by the guerrillas as they fled the scene.

On the basis of the exhumation results and the testimony of villagers who recognized several soldiers involved in the operation in San Francisco, Judge Pena ordered the arrest of four soldiers on October 13.[184] The judge also ordered the military to supply a more complete report on the men involved in the operation. (Officers had initially supplied a list of 33 names without information on rank or assignments.) Of four soldiers ordered detained by the judge, only one appeared on the list provided by the Fifth Brigade.[185]

On October 19, the judge forwarded undisclosed items to the Commission's forensic unit for testing. According to the State Department's biannual "Report on the Situation in El Salvador," President Duarte "authorized a separate inquiry by the Special Investigative Unit (SIU)" in late October 1988,[186] one month after the killings occurred. Yet a U.S. Embassy official told a Lawyers Committee representative that the Justice Minister did not actually order the SIU inquiry until November 16, 1988.

Six weeks later -- with the military still refusing to comply with the detention order[187] -- Judge Pena resigned his post. He

---

[184]Interviews with U.S. Embassy and the Attorney General's office. See also *The Washington Post*, October 14, 1988.

[185]Interview with U.S. Embassy official, November 2, 1988.

[186]The Department of State, "Report on the Situation in El Salvador," December 1, 1988, pursuant to Section 561 of Public Law 100-202, p.15.

[187]The Ministry of Defense said it could not comply with the detention order because it had never received the requisite copy of the document. The Lawyers Committee has learned that the judge

had actually secretly tendered his resignation weeks earlier as he left the country on an authorized leave of absence, a U.S. Embassy source told the Lawyers Committee. On February 4, Judge Edis Alcides Guandique was appointed to succeed Judge Pena.

U.S. Pressure Continues

To emphasize the importance U.S. officials attributed to the San Francisco massacre, Vice President Dan Quayle was sent to El Salvador on February 3 to raise State Department concerns about this and other human rights violations. Quayle was reported to have turned over a list of three Fifth Brigade officers believed responsible for the killings.[188]

On February 13 -- four months after the detention order was issued -- three of the four soldiers named in the detention order entered pleas of innocence with the court; the fourth also later pleaded innocent. The judge ordered that one body be exhumed for a second time in order to determine the caliber of bullet.[189]

U.S. Ambassador William Walker visited Judge Edis Alcides Guandique in his San Sebastian office on February 17, expressing U.S. support for his efforts to prosecute those responsible.[190] Yet the case did not appear to be progressing, and on February 25, *The Washington Post* reported that "despite public assurances to the contrary, no investigation of the killings is underway."

By early March, the military had changed its version of events, admitting that the 10 peasants had been killed by Fifth Brigade members, who then misled their commanding officers about the incident. Three officers -- Maj. Mauricio de Jesus Beltran, Lt. Arnoldo Antonio Vasquez, and Lt. Manuel de Jesus Galvez Galvez

---

signed but never issued the orders, instructing his secretary not to act on them.

[188]*Los Angeles Times*, March 9, 1989.

[189]*El Diario de Hoy*, February 14, 1989.

[190]*Washington Post*, March 9, 1989.

-- were placed under arrest at San Salvador's National Guard headquarters.[191] An Armed Forces communique said four soldiers were also consigned to the courts, and absolved Col. Emilio Chavez Caceres -- the *tandona* member who heads the Fifth Brigade -- from all responsibility.[192] The press release placed blame for the massacre on Maj. Beltran, an intelligence officer.

Invoking language used in earlier human rights cases, U.S. Ambassador William Walker said San Francisco was a test case for Salvadoran justice:

> I consider it the key case as yet unresolved, which must be resolved if El Salvador wants to show the world it's serious about the investigation of alleged rights violations.[193]

On March 9, 1989, the *Los Angeles Times* reported:

> Sources close to the military say the action in the San Sebastian case is little more than a sop to pacify the United States and that Quayle's message is being largely disregarded.

---

[191]*Washington Post*, March 9, 1989.

[192]*La Prensa Grafica*, March 13, 1989; *El Diario de Hoy*, March 13, 1989. Earlier reports indicated that Col. Chavez Caceres had been suspended from his command. See *Los Angeles Times*, March 9, 1989. *Tandona* is the name given to the large group of officers who graduated from El Salvador's military academy in 1966. A graduating class is known as a *tanda* and *tandona* indicates a large *tanda*. These officers dominate the Armed Forces today, holding some 23 key leadership positions.

[193] *Washington Post*, March 9, 1989.

The wife of Manuel de Jesus Santamaria, a Puerta del Diablo victim,
at their home in San Jose Guayabal, August 1988.
(Photo: Corinne Dufka)

Killings at Puerta del Diablo
January 31, 1988

The tortured bodies of Jose Luis Cornejo Calles, 27, Jose Javier Santamaria, 14, and Miguel Angel Santamaria Raymundo, 27, were discovered by a tourist on February 1, 1988 in a parking lot at the Devil's Gate Park in Planes de Renderos on the outskirts of San Salvador.[194] In the early 1980's when the death count reached some 800 per month, *Puerta del Diablo* was a frequent dumping ground for many victims of death squad killings.

The bodies, as yet unidentified, were judicially recognized at 6:30 p.m. by the Justice of the Peace of Panchimalco. The thumbs of the two older men were tied together; the head of 14-year-old Javier Santamaria was "semidestroyed" by a gun blast. All showed "signs of torture" but had been executed by M-16s and another 38-calibre weapon.[195]

The Detention

The three were picked up about 10:00 p.m. on January 31, 1988 as they made their way home to the village of Melendez from a festival in the nearby town of San Jose Guayabal. The three were stopped separately by armed men, some in civilian clothes and some in the uniform of the PRAL unit of the First Infantry Brigade in San Salvador. PRAL is an elite Long Range Patrol set up and trained with U.S. assistance.[196]

---

[194]*El Diario de Hoy*, February 2, 1988. Devil's Gate Park is known in Spanish as *la Puerta del Diablo*.

[195]Court documents reviewed by the Lawyers Committee, September 29, 1988, Third Penal Court of San Salvador; *La Prensa Grafica*, February 2, 1988; Tutela, Investigacion Judicial, February 2, 1988.

[196]Account based on *Washington Post*, February 8, 1988; Tutela #020288, Investigacion In Sito, Panchimalco, February 2, 1988; Tutela, Conclusiones de la investigacion de las tres personas capturadas en San Jose Guayabal y Encontradas en la Puerta del Diablo; Investigacion Judicial, February 2, 1988, Juzgado de Paz, Panchimalco, San Salvador; Tutela #02144; 02146; 02147; 02145.

Among their captors was a guerrilla deserter known to area residents as "Tony." In the period preceding the killings, Tony had been seen wearing a military uniform and working with the First Brigade. Residents describe him as a brown-haired man in his mid-twenties, who is approximately 1 meter 70 cm tall. Reportedly, he has limited use of fingers on his right hand.[197]

According to the testimony of Marta Dinora Melgar, widow of Jose Luis Cornejo, and a young friend of Javier Santamaria -- both of whom were detained and later released -- the armed men asked to see personal identification.[198] According to their testimonies, the armed men seemed to be looking particularly for the three victims.

The Aftermath

Because of the location where the corpses were found, the Devil's Gate deaths were widely reported at home and abroad.[199] Auxiliary Bishop Gregorio Rosa Chavez of the Archdiocese of San Salvador denounced the killings on February 7 during a portion of the weekly homily known as The Week's Happenings. Saying he was "horrified" by the documentation of 26 "violent deaths" during the last week by Tutela Legal -- several of them excessively cruel -- the bishop placed responsibility for some of these murders directly on the First Brigade's PRAL.[200]

Bishop Rosa Chavez was subsequently instructed to appear on three separate occasions by Third Penal Judge Lic. Juan Hector Larios Larios. The judge challenged him to provide proof of PRAL culpability. In a written response to Larios, Rosa Chavez said he

---

[197]Acto de Declaracion de Testigo, February 13, 1988, before Third Penal Judge, San Salvador, by Hector Salvador Ardon Guerrero and Javier Francisco Melendez.

[198]Tutela Legal, #02144, February 12, 1988.

[199]See for example, *La Prensa Grafica*, February 2, 1988; *El Diario de Hoy*, February 2, 1988 *El Mundo*, March 4, 1988; *Washington Post*, February 2, 1988.

[200]*Orientacion*, February 14, 1988, Homilia de Monsenor Gregorio Rosa Chavez, Obispo Auxiliar de San Salvador, en la Catedral Metropolitana, pp.2 and 11.

had been called at home by Chief of Staff Gen. Adolfo Blandon.[201] Rosa Chavez also provided a transcription and audio cassette of the February 7, 1988 sermon and said he could not provide the court with copies of testimony taken by Tutela Legal without the witnesses' permission. The Bishop pointed out that the court had already taken statements from some of the same deponents and therefore had access to the same evidence.[202]

On February 11, President Duarte went on Salvadoran television to blast the Church for "again going to the pulpit to make charges."[203] In a Lawyers Committee interview on October 4, 1988, Judge Larios accused Rosa Chavez of acting "capriciously. He wanted to provoke a needless confrontation between the Church and the judicial system."[204]

---

[201]Article 205 of the Criminal Procedure Code allows for written testimony from certain categories of citizens, among them, bishops.

[202]Court documents #79-84, April 30, 1988, Third Penal Court, San Salvador.

[203]On February 11, 1988 Channel Six broadcast the following remarks on the *Puerta del Diablo* case by Duarte: "The Church is again going to the pulpit to make charges. There are three deaths that must be investigated. However, the bad thing about this is that they have taken sides. The bad thing is that they are making statements about things that have not been proven. If they blame someone, they should prove it first. Before doing or saying such things they should follow the judicial process to prove his statements. I believe Msgr. Gregorio Rosa Chavez and his legal advisor should give testimony to a judge, because if he is certain that soldiers of the First Brigade were the ones who carried out those assassinations, he must therefore have some proof. Thus, he should provide it. He should assume responsibility." FBIS-LAT-88-029, February 12, 1988.

[204]The polemic between the judiciary and the Church continued for some time. Denouncing the "sand-digger" deaths, Auxiliary Bishop Gregorio Rosa Chavez said in the homily on April 24, 1988 that he found it "grotesque that those who are supposed to investigate (the authorities) call on us to do it ourselves...one has the right to say this is bad and that it is the responsibility of the organs of justice to do the investigations." As cited in *El Mundo*, April 25, 1988.

The Investigation

In light of the testimony implicating the First Brigade as well as the detailed physical description of former guerrilla "Tony," the court requested the military to provide the names and ranks of those on patrol in the area that day. Vice Minister of Defense Gen. Rafael Flores Lima responded on May 27, 1988, appending a list of 339 soldiers, 43 of whom were named Antonio.[205]

Lic. Arturo Lazo of the Human Rights Department of the Attorney General's office told the Lawyers Committee on July 11, 1988 that since his unit had no investigative capacity, he had asked the collaboration of the SIU. A list of SIU cases provided by Justice Minister Julio Samayoa does not mention the case, however, and Dr. Samayoa confirmed in a Lawyers Committee interview on July 15, 1988 that the SIU had not looked into the deaths.

Lazo acknowleged the lack of progress in this investigation in a July Lawyers Committee interview, noting that there were no suspects. "I can't go to the First Brigade and ask to see every soldier named Tony with a defect on his right hand. They just wouldn't let me."

Interviewed again in September, Lic. Lazo said there had been no progress. "It's problematic. What are we going to do? To be honest, there's little hope that this case will progress."[206]

In October, Judge Larios said that having just completed another complicated case, he intended to focus on the *Puerta del Diablo* killings, beginning by sifting through the list of potential military suspects.

As of January 1989, there were no developments in the case and the SIU had still not launched an investigation.

---

[205]Documents reviewed by Lawyers Committee, September 29, 1988, Third Penal Court.

[206]Lawyers Committee interview, San Salvador, September 27, 1988.

Florinda Rivera, 44, at the grave of her son, Mario Cruz Rivera, shortly before the exhumation at Tepemechin, May 24, 1988. (photo: Corinne Dufka)

Felix Antonio Rivera and Mario Cruz Rivera
February 26, 1988

Detention, Torture, and Murders

On February 25, 1988, uniformed soldiers attached to Military Outpost Number Four (*Destacamento Militar Numero Cuatro*) based in San Francisco Gotera entered the community of Tepemechin, village of El Tablon, jurisdiction of Sociedad, department of Morazan. Commanded at the time by Col. Juan Carlos Carrillo Schlencker, Outpost Number Four is under the jurisdiction of the Third Infantry Brigade at San Miguel, then headed by Col. Rene Emilio Ponce, the *tandona* leader who was named Chief of Staff in November 1988.

Maria Juana Gomez Granados, 17, was accompanying the soldiers. She had been captured earlier in Quezaltepeque, department of La Libertad by the National Police. After they discovered she lacked identity papers, the police transported her to her home community. According to the testimony of a neighbor, Gomez, the former girlfriend of one of the victims, was armed and uniformed.[207]

Around midnight the men knocked on the door of Sebastian Gutierrez, calling, "Sebastian, the guerrillas are talking to you." Gutierrez, 18, went outside, barefoot and clothed only in his underwear. Searching the home for weapons, the soldiers beat the elder Gutierrez, Alvaro, and Sebastian's wife, Alejandra Bonilla, who had given birth six days earlier. Finding nothing, they went off with Sebastian in tow.

That morning around 2:00, the men arrived at the home of Felix Antonio Rivera, 25, a member of the 15th of September Cooperative, affiliated with the Association of Democratic Indigenous Salvadorans (ASID).[208] Rivera and his father, 65-year-old Santos Gonzalez, were beaten as the men ransacked the house,

---

[207]Tutela Legal #02185

[208]ASID members are primarily indigenous peasants, many of whom are organized into co-ops. ASID is part of the National Peasant Union (UNC), which is affiliated with the opposition UNTS.

tearing up a bank note, their personal identity documents, and a deed for the family plot issued by the Salvadoran National Financial Institute (FINATA), a governmental institution.[209] Santos Gonzalez died a few days after the beating by members of Outpost Number Four.

The 50-year-old father of the third detainee, Mario Cruz Rivera, told Tutela Legal[210] that he had just arrived home from work when a soldier burst through his door asking for 16-year-old Mario, also a co-op member. Informed that Mario would be home in the morning after his all-night shift at the sugar mill, the soldiers searched the house "for weapons," tearing up the man's new ID and some bank papers. According to the father's account, he was held face down on the floor at gunpoint, threatened with death if he got up. Mario was immediately tied up when he arrived at 6:00 a.m., and as he was led off his father saw that Sebastian Gutierrez and Felix Antonio Rivera had already been detained.

Residents in the neighboring village, El Ocotillo, testified that they saw the three bound men in the soldiers' custody. The group then walked back toward El Tablon, arriving at a mill near the Tepemechin river. The *hacienda* owner says the soldiers, who arrived around 11:00 a.m., beat his workers and accused them of being guerrillas.

The armed men left about 11:30 a.m. and about two blocks from the *hacienda,* set fire to a field and forced the three barefoot captives to run through. At a nearby washstand or *pila,* Mario Cruz Rivera and Felix Antonio Rivera were killed. There were no eyewitnesses to the murders, but the *hacienda* owner heard the men's screams and gunshots. Soldiers attempted to simulate a skirmish and called in a helicopter to bomb the area.[211]

---

[209]Accounts of the detentions and deaths are based on interviews conducted by the Lawyers Committee in Morazan in February 1988; with family members and other witnesses on March 25; and on testimony taken by Tutela Legal.

[210]Tutela Legal, #02275, March 24, 1988.

[211]This account appears in a summary of the case prepared for the Lawyers Committee, based on interviews in Morazan and San Salvador, February-March 1988.

At about 1:30 p.m. the soldiers stopped at the home of Hector Garcia, 26, a resident of Varilla Negra, and told him not to be frightened when he went to the *pila*. Sebastian Gutierrez, still in custody, was led away with the soldiers and has not yet been located, despite repeated inquiries by the family and human rights workers.

Mario's father, informed by a neighbor of the location of the bodies, went to the washstand, later describing his son's condition to Tutela Legal:

> The cadaver had no ears; there were three stab wounds close together on the left side of the neck, although I'm not sure if they were all stab wounds or bullet holes; they had cut off the end of his nose; they had cut off his thumbs and the ring finger on his left hand. Felix Antonio was in much the same state.[212]

The two were buried on February 26 on a hillside near the washstand.

The Exhumation

With the help of the nongovernmental Human Rights Commission (CDHES), the families obtained an exhumation order from the First Instance Judge of San Francisco Gotera, Dr. Andres Pineda Chicas. In attendance on May 24 was a large delegation representing the governmental, nongovernmental, and foreign human rights communities; the foreign and domestic media; families and neighbors of the victims; and the justice system, including: five forensic technicians attached to the Special Investigative Unit (including a forensic pathologist); three members of the Human Rights Department of the *Fiscalia* or Attorney General's office; the Justice of the Peace of Corinto, Porfirio Benitez Gonzalez, and his secretary. [213]

---

[212]Tutela Legal, #02275, March 24, 1988.

[213]This account is based on the observations of two Lawyers Committee representatives who witnessed the exhumation at Varilla Negra on May 24, 1988.

The medical team consisted of Dr. Guillermo Armando Alvarado Moran of the SIU, Dr. Juan Antonio Leira, a fifth year medical student, and Dr. Jorgen Thomsen, a Danish forensic pathologist and member of the Committee of Concerned Forensic Scientists for the Documentation of Human Rights Abuses, who participated under the sponsorship of the Washington-based American Association for the Advancement of Science (AAAS).

Despite the SIU presence, the disinterment was conducted by human rights workers and neighbors.[214] The bodies were first sighted at 12:35 p.m., after nearly an hour and a half of digging, about one meter below the surface. The two were wrapped in one piece of plastic, serving to advance decomposition.

The head of Felix Antonio Rivera was "extensively shattered" and both thumbs were missing below the joint.[215] Several bones were broken, including a lower rib on the left side. Because of the advanced state of decomposition, it was impossible to detect burn marks on the feet or if the ears had been cut off. No bullet holes were observed. Dr. Thomsen concluded that several lesions resulted from "severe trauma, possibly by a blunt instrument. However, they may well have been caused by gunshots"; the fingers were likely severed by "sharp force" (e.g., a knife).

"None of the lesions could be the result of three months in an undisturbed grave. It could not be determined however, if the lesions were inflicted before or after death." Nor could the cause of death be "established with certainty."

Dr. Guillermo Alvarado Moran of the SIU opined that the cause of death was "multiple traumas, especially to the head, as well

---

[214]Dr. Alvarado's report to the SIU lists five participants from the SIU's "technical forensic unit." One of the five was a photographer. Only Dr. Alvarado, however, was observed taking an active role.

[215]These observations are taken from the report of Dr. Jorgen Thomsen to the American Association for the Advancement of Science.

as possible deep wounds caused by fire arms to the neck and armpit with concomitant profuse hemorrhaging." [216]

Due to the advanced state of decomposition, Dr. Thomsen was unable to detect gunshot or stab wounds in the body of 16-year-old Mario Rivera. He was able to confirm parts of the father's observations: missing fourth ring finger on left hand; both ears missing; tip of nose missing. Dr. Thomsen did not exclude the possibility that the missing ears and nose had resulted from deterioration of the corpses, but found it "more likely...that [they] were cut or chopped off before or after death."

In neither case was Dr. Thomsen able to establish the definitive cause of death or if the deceased had been tortured prior to death or mutilated after death.

Dr. Alvarado's brief report on Mario Cruz Rivera describes the same lesions, concluding that the cause of death was "possibly hemorrhaging due to gunshot wounds at the level of the neck and armpit."

Reactions

Interviewed in San Miguel on the evening of the exhumation, Col. Rene Emilio Ponce, since named to head the High Command of the Salvadoran Armed Forces, read reporters the battle report filed for February 26 indicating that two "subversives" had been killed in a firefight. Saying he would not investigate the slayings, Col. Ponce told *The Washington Post*:

> I do not know anything about other reports. If there was mutilation, it is reprehensible and should be condemned in every aspect. We cannot investigate every combat report. In these cases I must believe what my colonels report.[217]

The governmental Human Rights Commission denounced the killings in a paid advertisement in *El Mundo* on April 27, 1988.

---

[216]Report of Dr. Guillermo Alvarado to Lt. Col. Art. Dem. Nelson Ivan Lopez y Lopez, Jefe de la Unidad Ejecutiva, May 26, 1988.

[217]*The Washington Post*, June 12, 1988.

In his April 17, 1988 homily, Archbishop Arturo Rivera y Damas said that with each rights violation the government:

loses what little had been gained, and the pendulum swings toward the other extreme. This is not right; we are moving backward. Human rights violations had diminished, but now they are increasing.

Denouncing the spate of abuses in this area of Morazan, the Archbishop continued:

I ask the Army to stop regarding these people as guerrilla *masas* [civilian supporters of the guerrillas]. They have suffered too much. There have been four deaths and some disappearances among them, and they ask to be able to work without fear and in peace.[218]

The Investigation

Personnel from the Attorney General's office attended the exhumation on May 24, 1988 and Lic. Arturo Lazo confirmed in a Lawyers Committee interview on July 11 that his Human Rights Department was investigating these killings and others in this community. In September he said the case was still in the investigatory or *instruccion* phase and that his office was attempting -- so far unsuccessfully -- to identify those soldiers on patrol in the area on the day the men were detained.

Justice Minister Julio Samayoa said the SIU's involvement was limited to the autopsy conducted on the day of exhumation by Dr. Guillermo Alvarado Moran.[219]

To our knowledge, there has been no progress, and the Lawyers Committee has since learned that the judge with jurisdiction in the case has resigned and not yet been replaced.

In response to an October 1988 letter from nine U.S. Senators raising concerns about this and other human rights cases in El Salvador, the U.S. Embassy said that Sebastian Gutierrez, the

---

[218]As cited in *El Mundo*, April 18, 1988.

[219]Lawyers Committee interview with Dr. Samayoa, July 15, 1988.

third man detained with the two victims, remains disappeared. Concerning the killings of Felix Antonio Rivera and Mario Cruz Rivera, the Embassy said "The judicial investigation into the deaths remains incomplete due to the lack of the names of suspects."[220]

---

[220]Unclassified cable to Senator Mark O. Hatfield, November 22, 1988.

Jose Antonio Lopez Cruz , Jose Bertilio Alvarado Lopez,
and Jose Antonio Ortega Orellana
"Los Degollados"
Attempted Killings on June 13, 1987

In El Salvador, Jose Antonio Lopez Cruz, Jose Bertilio
Alvarado Lopez, and Jose Antonio Ortega Orellana are known
simply as *Los degollados*, those whose throats were slit. In Spanish,
degollar suggests slaughter by slitting the animal's throat. Unlike
many accounts of human rights violations, these Chalatenango case
histories are based on the victims' own testimony. Miraculously, the
three -- and a fourth man known simply as Mario -- lived to tell
their stories.

Jose Antonio Lopez Cruz

Jose Antonio Lopez Cruz, 28, has lived since birth in the
community of La Vega, village of Los Prados, jurisdiction of La
Laguna. He and his common-law wife, Dominga Lopez, have six
children. At the time of the attempted murder, Lopez Cruz, a small
farmer, had belonged to a low-income agricultural buying co-op for
two years.

On Saturday June 13, 1987 Lopez Cruz returned to his home
about 7:00 p.m. after attending a co-op meeting. His wife told him
that some soldiers had been patrolling the area, but had not talked
to anyone. The whole family went to bed around 8:00 p.m. and
were awakened about 1:00 a.m. by shouting through an open
window. When they realized that those ordering them to get out of
bed were soldiers, the couple and some of their children went
outside. In front of the house were several uniformed soldiers,
some of whom had also detained Lopez Cruz' 18-year-old brother
and mother, who lived nearby. Both family groups were taken to
the home of Mario and his wife, Delmi, who had recently moved to
the neighborhood. Lopez Cruz estimates that there were some 25
uniformed, armed soldiers.[221]

The men were taken out of hearing distance, and ultimately
away from the houses, where the interrogation began. According to
Lopez Cruz' testimony, he was questioned by two short, stout
soldiers in camouflage. The soldiers asked him where he kept his

---

[221]Declaracion del ofendido Jose Antonio Lopez Cruz, First
Instance Court, Dulce Nombre de Maria, August 14, 1987.

weapons and to confirm that he was a guerrilla. The victim insisted he could not answer because he knew nothing, to which one soldier responded, "Since you won't tell us about the weapons, you're going to have to die."

The other soldier asked, "How shall he be killed, with the *corvo* [a curved, machete-like farming implement] or with a gun?" They agreed on the *corvo*, which one of them obtained from a group of soldiers nearby. The victim was ordered to lie face down. He protested that he should not be killed for something he did not know, but finally did as he was told, at gunpoint.

Lopez Cruz was slashed three times in the back of the neck. When the soldiers heard him breathing a few moments later, he heard one say, "You're still not dead yet!" The *corvo* was then plunged into his shoulder, and manipulated back and forth to deepen the wound. Next the *corvo* was entered into a previous wound, which was extended around toward the throat. Lopez Cruz testified that he knew he was losing a lot of blood and then passed out, for about two hours, he believes.

Regaining consciousness, Lopez Cruz made his way home, which is inaccessible by car. With the assistance of family and friends, the victim walked two hours and was ultimately driven to San Salvador's Rosales Hospital. When his wife came to visit on Sunday June 21, she told him that she had been raped by five soldiers in olive green camouflage who had been in the group which detained him. Pregnant at the time of the rape, Dominga Lopez subsequently gave birth to a very small premature baby.[222]

Mario, slashed that same night, fled to Honduras after briefly visiting his wife Delmi, who was also raped. According to

---

[222]Lawyers Committee interviews, November 18 and December 29-30, 1987, La Laguna, Chalatenango.
Dominga Lopez Rivera made her declaration to the judge in Dulce Nombre de Maria on August 14, 1987. Lopez Rivera said that after her husband was taken away, six soldiers removed her from her house, called her husband a "terrorist," repeatedly asked where he kept his weapons, and threatened her with a *corvo*. Five of the soldiers then raped her, one after the other. In her statement to the court, the victim said that the moonlight was strong that night, and that she could identify her attackers. Declaracion de la Ofendida, Dominga Lopez Rivera, August 14, 1987, First Instance Court, Dulce Nombre de Maria.

testimony taken by Tutela Legal on June 16, 1987, Delmi, pregnant at the time, miscarried shortly after the rape.[223]

Jose Antonio Ortega Orellana

Jose Antonio Ortega Orellana, 26, was stopped by soldiers of the Belloso Battalion at 3:00 or 4:00 p.m. on Saturday, June 13. Ortega was on the road from La Cuchilla to his mother's home in Canton Plan Verde. A farmer and day laborer, Ortega was active in the local Catholic parish and had studied to become a health promoter. Ortega and his common-law wife have no children.

Approximately 15 to 20 soldiers, dressed in green fatigues or camouflage, walked Ortega toward Plan Verde, stopping at a cemetery. Taking Ortega off to the side, three soldiers questioned him about where he kept weapons and the names of his guerrilla comrades.

The three encircled him, saying that "since he did not want to say anything, they were going to kill him." One took out his dagger and stabbed Ortega repeatedly in the throat. Weakened by the loss of blood, he felt his left arm lose strength, and eventually dropped to the ground. Ortega later felt a boot on his chest and his head was lifted by the left ear. He made an effort not to breathe. Convinced that he was dead, the attackers left.

Ortega says he tried twice unsuccessfully to get up. Finally he was able to hail a passerby whom he knew about 6:30 a.m. The victim was carried in a hammock to the house of his mother, and eventually transported to San Salvador.[224]

---

[223]Tutela Legal, #01366, #01393; Lawyers Committee interviews with the three victims in Rosales, and with the brother of Lopez Cruz, San Salvador, June 18, 1988; summary of the cases prepared for the Lawyers Committee, June 18, 1987.

[224]Lawyers Committee interview with Ortega Orellana in Rosales Hospital; Tutela Legal #01366 and #01369.

Jose Bertilio Alvarado Lopez

Jose Bertilio Alvarado Lopez, 28, arrived at his home in Canton La Chuchilla, jurisdiction La Laguna, about 4:00 p.m. on June 13, 1987, after working in his bean patch. At home were his wife, Maria Ana Gloria Menjivar and their two children, Maria Sara Alvarado, 2, and two-month-old Jose Ovidio Alvarado. Alvarado is an active catechist, often assisting during mass.

Four men in fatigues -- one sergeant, one corporal, and two soldiers -- carrying M-16s asked his name and said they would like to question him. Alvarado Lopez later told Tutela Legal that the men said they were attached to the garrison at El Paraiso, Chalatenango.[225] They took him about 25 meters from his house and accused him of being a guerrilla, which he denied. Leading him to the cemetery -- where other members of the Armed Forces had gathered -- they interrogated him further and took his identity papers from him. The sergeant then ordered the others to kill him, "because he didn't want to give them the weapons." One soldier pulled a dagger from his belt and stabbed Alvarado twice in the throat and a third time on the left side of the neck. He was found by the friends of Ortega Orellana and also taken to San Salvador. Alvarado Lopez was operated on that same night at Rosales.[226]

The Aftermath

Mario has returned from Honduras and is again living in Chalatenango with his wife. Jose Bertilio Alvarado Lopez is living in a canton in Los Prados, jurisdiction of La Laguna. Jose Antonio Lopez Cruz has returned to La Laguna with his wife Dominga. Jose Antonio Ortega Orellana remained for a time at the Church-run San Jose Calle Real Refugee Camp in Apopa, where he was taken after his release from Rosales Hospital. According to an examining physician, he has never regained normal use of his left arm, which was injured in the incident.

---

[225]Tutela Legal #01370. The Fourth Infantry Brigade was then under the command of Col. Jose Humberto Gomez, a *tandona* member who now heads the National Guard.

[226]Tutela Legal #01379; Lawyers Committee interview, June 18, 1987.

The Investigation

Questioned about the attacks, an Armed Forces spokesman told *The New York Times* that none of his personnel were involved.[227] President Duarte pledged to investigate and the case was referred to the Special Investigative Unit. According to information provided to the Lawyers Committee by the Minister of Justice, Dr. Julio Alfredo Samayoa, the case was suspended without action.[228]

According to the victims' testimony, their attackers were members of the Fourth Brigade or the U.S.-trained Belloso Battalion under the command of Lt. Col. Ricardo Antonio Martinez Cuellar.[229] On August 20, 1987, the Judge of First Instance in Dulce Nombre, Dora del Carmen Gomez de Claros, requested that the Fourth Brigade provide names and assignments of those troops on patrol in La Laguna from June 1-30, 1987. A few months later, the Brigade answered that during the month of June men from the Cobra, Cayaguanca and the Ramon Belloso Battalion had all operated in La Laguna; no further information was provided.

Lic. Arturo Lazo, head of the Human Rights department in the Attorney General's office, said his unit is working on the case, which is in the investigation [*instruccion*] phase. Since there are no individuals implicated, amnesty has not been requested, and Lazo had "nothing concrete" to report.[230]

---

[227]*New York Times*, June 19, 1987.

[228]*Nomina de Casos Asignados a la unidad ejecutiva de la comision de investigacion de hechos delictivos*, San Salvador, July 14, 1988. The statement on the case reads in its entirety: "The three men were captured by individuals who presumably belong to the Armed Forces, of unknown identity, since no one has supplied information on them." A list of SIU cases was provided to the Lawyers Committee during an interview with Justice Minister Samayoa on July 15, 1988, San Salvador.

[229]*New York Times*, June 22, 1987. Several of the testimonies contained in a summary of court documents reviewed by the Lawyers Committee mention the Fourth Brigade. The file covers the period August 1987 to September 1988.

[230]Lawyers Committee interview with Arturo Lazo, July 11 and September 27, 1988, San Salvador.

Court documents reviewed by the Lawyers Committee indicate that the victims were interviewed in late June 1987 by Justices of the Peace in San Salvador. All three victims and over 15 witnesses subsequently filed declarations with the judge in Dulce Nombre. Telephoned on January 16, 1989, the court secretary in Dulce Nombre told the Lawyers Committee that while the case was still open, there had been no progress. Harassed in connection with another case, Judge Gomez de Claros has applied for permission to emigrate to Canada.[231]

---

[231]*San Francisco Examiner*, December 11, 1988. Judge Gomez de Claros encountered difficulties with the Fourth Brigade after she re-opened the investigation into the killings of four Dutch journalists in March 1982.

The Palitos Well Case
May 21, 1987

The Killings

Jose Pilar Serafin Rivera Romero, 26; Miguel Angel Cristino Machado Argueta, 32; Santiago Coreas, 23; Jose Candelario Rodriquez, 22; Andres Mejia Roque, 32; were all recruited by the Popular Revolutionary Army (ERP) to carry out tasks for the guerrillas on or about May 18, 1987. The men and their families were told that the tasks would take about three days and that they would then be free to return home. It is not known if the five willingly cooperated with the guerrillas, though some had previously carried out missions, which often consist of carrying food, weapons, or supplies for the movement.[232]

Returning from their assignment, the five were apprehended by members of the elite U.S.-trained Arce Batallion then under the command of Col. Mauricio Staben.[233]   Residents say the Arce

---

[232]This account is based on research and interviews conducted by the Lawyers Committee in June and July 1987 in El Salvador as well as the testimonies of the mothers of two of the victims recorded by Tutela Legal on June 5, 1987 in the department of San Miguel.

[233]Col. Mauricio Staben, a member of the large 1966 graduating class of the military academy known as the *tandona*, was recently transferred from his post at the head of the Arce Battalion to the top spot at Military Outpost Seven in Ahuachapan. In 1986, Col. Staben stalled for a month before complying with a military summons to turn himself in for questioning in connection with the kidnapping-for-profit case. He was released without having been interrogated when fellow *tandona* officers pleaded his case with the Attorney General. On May 7, President Duarte reinstated him to his command, saying "There is no evidence to detain him." Staben was implicated by three other suspects, including Lopez Sibrian, still detained in connection with the case.

On June 22, 1987, *The New York Times* reported that Staben "is believed by American officials to have overseen the killing of perhaps hundreds of people suspected of being leftists in the past....Colonel Staben has denied the charges, but he is one of the most feared men in the military and the Arce Battalion is regularly cited as the leading abuser of human rights among army units." Until 1984, Staben commanded the barracks next to *El Playon*,

entered the zone from the direction of Sensuntepeque in the department of Cabanas and came upon the unarmed men around Palitos, jurisdiction Nuevo Eden de San Juan, department of San Miguel.

While witnesses saw the men in military custody, no one actually saw the killings and there are several versions of how the five were detained and the circumstances of their death. A press release put out by the Press Committee of the Armed Forces of El Salvador (COPREFA) on May 22, 1987 reports that "five terrorists died in combat with military forces of the Arce Batallion" which was on a "search operation" [rastreo] in the hamlet of San Andres, Nuevo Eden de San Juan.[234] That version promptly turned up in San Salvador's two leading morning papers.[235]

The families learned from Palitos residents that the five men had been detained on May 20, questioned and held overnight in a chapel known as "the hermitage," and shot the next morning.

These witnesses say they heard shooting and later saw blood around the well, noticing too that dirt had been disturbed and branches cut off nearby trees. Down the deep shaft could be seen the outlines of bodies covered with earth and branches.

The Judicial Process and Public Reaction

In July 1987, family members filed a criminal complaint against the Arce Battalion before Dr. Augusto Antonio Romero Barrios, Judge of First Instance in Ciudad Barrios. Dr. Romero also issued summonses for two witnesses to the events. Apparently apprised of the judicial proceedings, the Arce again moved into the area, threatening those who dared to testify with death, according

---

notorious dumping ground for the death squads. See Jefferson Morley, "Salvador Justice: The Curious Case of Colonel Staben," *The New Republic*, September 8, 1986.

[234]Comite de Prensa de la Fuerza Armada, San Salvador, May 22, 1987, "FMLN Secuestra y Asesina Campesinos."

[235]*El Diario de Hoy*, May 23, 1987, pp. 6 and 47 and *La Prensa Grafica*, May 23, 1987, pp. 5 and 17.

to the testimonies of area residents. Soldiers also tampered with the well site, which the families, who considered it a grave, had decorated with crosses and flowers.

When the families returned to Judge Romero in late July, a lawyer representing the Arce Battalion attempted to dissuade them from proceeding with the case. Several witnesses who initially told their stories to family members and human rights monitors who visited the area, later denied that they had seen or heard anything.

In the Sunday homily on June 7, 1987, Msgr. Arturo Rivera y Damas, Archbishop of San Salvador, challenged the military to investigate the case:

> We have amply documented reports, according to which five young collaborators of the FMLN in the jurisdiction of Nuevo Eden de San Juan, San Miguel, died at the hands of members of the Arce Battalion, who threw the bodies into a well. The High Command should intervene in this matter.[236]

On June 20, San Salvador daily *El Diario de Hoy*, citing sources in the Arce Battalion, said that "Five *campesinos* who appeared dead in a well in Canton Palitos de Nuevo Eden de San Juan, San Miguel were assassinated and thrown into this place by terrorists of the so-called 'Revolutionary Army of the People' (ERP) and not by members of the Army." The article goes on to say that peasants had been coached into laying blame on the Arce by a Venezuelan "technician in psychological warfare with experience in Venezuela and Nicaragua...sent [to El Savador] by Moscow."[237]

An article appearing in late July said the ERP was threatening area residents with death if they did not abandon their homes.[238]

---

[236]Homilia del Domingo 7 de Junio de 1987, Mons. Arturo Rivera Damas.

[237]*El Diario de Hoy*, June 20, 1987, pp. 60 and 17.

[238]*La Prensa Grafica*, July 23, 1987, p. 27.

The Exhumation

Though the U.S. Embassy told the Lawyers Committee in July 1987 that the case had been sent to the Special Investigative Unit, the bodies were exhumed on July 28 without the benefit of the SIU's professional expertise. Over 100 members of the press, human rights and judicial communities were present during the more than six-hour process. In addition to Judge Romero Barrios were two local prosecutors (*fiscal de planta* and *fiscal especifico*) and Carlos Mendoza Burgos, an attorney for the Arce Battalion.[239]

Bits and pieces of the corpses -- handed to the surface after two hours of digging by a man standing on the muddy bottom -- were examined by Dr. Juan Bautista Chavez, forensic doctor in Ciudad Barrios.[240] The doctor found that four of the five had died "execution-style," since their skulls had been destroyed. He concluded that the throat of the fifth man had been slit.

Pieces of clothing and shoes enabled the families to identify the victims. Also brought to the surface were four plastic ponchos -- of the type used by the Armed Forces of El Salvador -- serving as shrouds. The remains were reburied in a common grave nearby.

The Amnesty

In a televised press conference on the day after the exhumation, Col. Mauricio Staben offered the military's third version of the killings, asserting that the Fifth Company of Riflemen ambushed a column of FMLN combatants near Palitos, killing five. Explaining why no weapons were recovered, Staben said other guerrillas had immediately retrieved them and probably thrown the bodies into the well, since the Arce had not done so.

---

[239]A representative of the Lawyers Committee attended the exhumation.

[240]The Lawyers Committee has learned that the volunteer who conducted the disinterment later fell seriously ill. He received no previous innoculations and drank liquor throughout the process, having to rest at one point because he was close to passing out.

The Palitos well case is listed among the SIU's suspended investigations. The document provided to the Lawyers Committee in July 1988 reads: "Information has been obtained that elements of the Arce Battalion, San Miguel, participated in the capture of these persons, but there are no eyewitnesses to the assassinations."[241]

Judge Romero requested the names of those men on patrol in Nuevo Eden de San Juan on the day of the killings. The Arce Battalion provided a list of over 50 soldiers, led by a lieutenant who had since died in combat.

In early April 1988, Judge Romero amnestied the case, citing the "20 or more provision" in the amnesty law.[242]

---

[241]*Nomina de Casos Asignados a la Unidad Ejecutiva de la Comision de Investigacion de Hechos Delictivos.*

[242]Article one of the law grants amnesty for crimes committed by more than 20 people, a catch-all provision designed to cover troops on patrol.

The Soyapango Sand-diggers
April 14, 1988

The Killings

Jose Arnoldo Cerritos, 25, was at home with his wife, children aged three and eight months, and his wife's uncle, Vicente Cerritos Torres, 56, on April 14, 1988 when three men in olive green uniforms came to their house about 7:30 p.m. The men told Maria Luisa Leiva Navarro, Cerritos' 19-year-old common-law wife, to put out the light and asked for her husband by name. When Cerritos came to the door, they grabbed him, tied him up and took him and the older man away, as she watched. One of the three captors stayed behind for five minutes to prohibit her from following.[243]

Arturo Navarro Garcia, cousin of Maria Luisa Leiva Navarro, was captured that same evening as he returned from digging sand about 7:45 p.m. with his helper, Manuel de Jesus Lopez Ramos, 18.[244] The two were stopped a few meters from Navarro Garcia's home by two armed men in uniform and ordered to lie face down on the ground. "Are you Arturo Navarro?" one soldier asked. When the victim said he was, the soldier replied, "Then you're coming with us." Lopez Ramos was allowed to leave, but had only gone a short distance when they called him back and searched his belongings before letting him go.

Higinia Sorto, Navarro Garcia's common-law wife who was interviewed in Vista Hermosa by the Lawyers Committee on May 21, 1988, said she was at an evangelical meeting that evening when her 9-year-old son, Rosendo Sorto Navarro, came to announce her husband's capture.

The Vista Hermosa community in Soyapango clings to the parched, barren bank of the River Canas, waterless during the dry season. It is largely populated by war refugees from the department

---

[243]Testimony of Maria Luisa Leiva Navarro taken by the Lawyers Committee, April 21, 1988 at the exhumation.

[244]Based on a summary of the case prepared for the Lawyers Committee, April 28, 1988; Lawyers Committee interview with victim's wife, Higinia Sorto, Soyapango, May 21, 1988; and Sorto's statement to Tutela Legal, #02363.

of Cabanas. Although the community is 12 years old, residents told the Lawyers Committee, most have settled there in the last six years. The community of some 25 families housed in shacks known as *champas* is adjacent to a development of solidly built block houses, yet Vista Hermosa remains without water, electricity, a school, or clinic. Unable to farm on the sandy, steep slopes, the community supports itself by gathering sand in the river bed. The sand -- used in construction -- is extracted with shovels and carried in sacks on the backs of local men, who then bargain with truckers serving as middlemen.

The Search

That same evening, the two wives inquired in vain about their husbands' whereabouts at Soyapango's Municipal Police and Civil Defense post. The next day, April 15, the two continued their search at the Air Force, the National Guard, the National Police, the Treasury Police, the Municipal Police, the El Zapote Garrison, the San Carlos Garrison and the headquarters of the Belloso Battalion in San Bartolo, Ilopango. In their statement to the court, the women said that an Air Force sergeant placed a call inquiring about the men by name.[245] After hanging up, he told them he thought they were there at the base and the women should wait. Three young armed men in civilian clothes later came out and told the women that their husbands were not at the Ilopango Air Base.

The next day, neighbors told the women that TV news had reported the discovery of three unidentified cadavers some 30 kilometers away in the department of La Paz. Family members learned in San Juan Talpa that the bodies had been hastily buried on April 16, 1988 without identification. According to a report from the Justice of the Peace, they were found in a 12-meter deep ditch along the road from Zacatecoluca to San Salvador, in an "advanced state of decomposition."[246] Fresh blood was found near the bodies, as well as two spent 45-calibre bullets, leading investigators to believe the men were murdered at the site.

---

[245]The widows made their judicial declarations to the court on April 21, 1988, at the exhumation. They were also interviewed on that day by governmental and nongovernmental human rights workers.

[246]Recopiliacion de datos de la investigacion judicial, April 18, 1988, Juzgado de Paz de San Juan Talpa, La Paz.

With the help of Tutela Legal, the legal aid office of the Catholic Archdiocese of San Salvador, and other human rights organizations, the families obtained an exhumation order from the Justice of the Peace in the town of San Juan Talpa.

The bodies were exhumed on April 21, with the aid of some local drunks, in the absence of trained technicians.[247] In attendance were the families of the three men, Tutela Legal, the nongovernmental and governmental Human Rights Commissions, a representative of Americas Watch and the Lawyers Committee, members of the Civil Defense and National Guard of San Juan Talpa, as well as the families of four other disappeared persons hoping to find their relatives. The Soyapango wives were able to identify their husbands, in one case only by the remains of his clothing since the exposed corpse had been partially eaten by buzzards.

The Possible Motive

According to residents' testimony, Vista Hermosa's sand-diggers became involved in late 1987 in a dispute with a nearby landowner over rights to the sand. The workers made contact with the National Association of Agricultural Workers (ANTA), which began organizing in the community in February 1988. An ANTA organizer told the Lawyers Committee that the association held meetings in Vista Hermosa every other week, and that two of the victims -- Arnoldo Cerritos and Arturo Navarro -- attended regularly. In early February a local TV station broadcast a segment about the dispute, interviewing community residents as well as the landowner. Community members said two of the men killed were visible in the group shown on television.

Residents say guerrillas do not pass through the community but that the Air Force, whose headquarters is located at nearby Ilopango Air Base, regularly patrol the area. One witness interviewed by U.S. free-lance journalist Frank Smythe said the

---

[247]On May 16, 1986, the Special Investigative Unit mobilized an impressive array of specialists to conduct a professional exhumation at the Armenia well. Salvadoran government souces told the Lawyers Committee that the SIU has conducted two other exhumations. Despite the existence of this professional know-how in El Salvador, subsequent exhumations have been carried out by volunteers or hirelings, who often seek fortification in alcohol. [On the Armenia well case, see p.34.]

captors wore the red beret which forms part of the Air Force uniform. Witnesses interviewed by Tutela Legal also mentioned the red beret.

The Investigation

The Human Rights Department of the Attorney General's office is investigating the case. Lic. Arturo Lazo of that office told the Lawyers Committee that testimonies have been taken from neighbors and family members. Lazo said available evidence was skimpy, and given that the men were detained at night it was difficult to find sufficient proof.[248] On September 27, Lic. Lazo said the sand-digger deaths were among those cases on which he was seeking SIU collaboration.[249] Justice Minister Julio Samayoa, who heads the Commission on Investigations, said the unit had not conducted an investigation because "no one had asked them to do so" and because "there are no witnesses." [250] A U.S. Embassy source confirmed in September 1988 that the SIU had not looked into the case.

Yet Dr. Samayoa's reasoning does not conform with the Commission's operating procedure, as specified in the law regulating the body and described by the Justice Minister himself during Lawyers Committee interviews on July 15 and September 14, 1988. The law stipulates that the Commission -- whose only voting members are the Vice Minister of the Interior, a representative of the President of the Republic, and the Justice Minister, who serves as chairman -- shall meet weekly and decide which cases to

---

[248]Lawyers Committee interview at the Attorney General's office, July 11, 1988.

[249]Lawyers Committee interview at the Attorney General's office, September 27, 1988.

[250]Lawyers Committee interview with Dr. Samayoa, at the SIU headquarters, San Salvador, July 15, 1988. Sources: Lawyers Committee on site investigation, May 21, 1988; Lawyers Committee summary of the case, April 28, 1988; Tutela Legal #02363, Recopilacion de datos de investigacion judicial segun juzgado de paz de San Juan Talpa, departamento de La Paz, April 18, 1988; Informe Especial, April 20, 1988, on visit to Justice of Peace with families to request exhumation; Informe especial, April 21, 1988, on the exhumation; La Prensa Grafica, April 18, 1988; El Mundo, April 18, 1988.

115

investigate. Cases are then referred to the Special Investigative Unit for action. Between meetings, the unit may launch an inquiry on its own while notifying the Commission within 72 hours. The Commission then has the right to suspend an investigation if it deems the inquiry unwarranted.[251]

---

[251]*Ley de Creacion de la Comision de Investigacion de Hechos Delictivos y Reglamento Especial de la Ley de Creacion de la Comision de Investigacion de Hechos Delictivos.* See page 41 for a discussion of the Commission on Investigations.

Adrian Chavarria Giron
April 29, 1988

The Killing

Adrian Chavarria Giron, 47, was stopped at a Treasury Police roadblock near the Unicentro shopping center in Soyapango, San Salvador department, about 7:30 p.m. on April 29, 1988, according to Danilo Umana, human rights secretary of the National Union of Workers and Peasants (UNOC).[252] His body was found early the next morning in Colonia Las Naves, Plan del Pino, the jurisdiction of Ciudad Delgado. His orange car was found about a kilometer from his body. The Justice of the Peace of Ciudad Delgado identified the body at 1:00 a.m. on April 30. Her report stated that Chavarria Giron's body had four bullet holes of unknown calibre.[253]

Chavarria Giron, a bus dispatcher, was the secretary of Domestic and International Relations of the General Confederation of Labor (CGT), a pro-PDC union group, and the treasurer of the Mutual Association of Bus Dispatchers (AMDT). At a press conference following the murder, a CGT official charged: "there is no doubt that he was assassinated by the Treasury Police."[254] According to the unionists' statement, he was forced to get out of his car and taken to another roadblock on the road to Tonacatepeque.

Rosa Lidia Perdomo, the victim's 35-year-old common law wife, told the human rights Office of the Archdiocese of San Salvador that her husband had never been threatened, and that she suspected the motive had been robbery. According to Perdomo, the following items were stolen at the time of the murder: $800 belonging to the AMDT; $100 of his own money; a 38-calibre

---

[252]Lawyers Committee interview with Danilo Umana, UNOC human rights director, January 12, 1988. UNOC is closely associated with the Christian Democratic Party (PDC).

[253]*El Mundo*, May 2, 1988; Tutela Legal, Recopilacion de datos de la investigacion judicial, May 9, 1988.

[254]*El Mundo*, May 2, 1988.

revolver; a watch; two gold rings; and a gold chain.[255] Danilo Umana, director of UNOC's newly formed human rights department, told the Lawyers Committee on January 12, 1989 that he believed the unionist's killers intended only to rob him, but after seeing his ID card decided they would have to kill him "because the CGT [the union to which the victim belonged] is an organization with a lot of respect in this country."

In the days following the murder, Chavarria Giron's automobile was held in the custody of the Treasury Police, who refused to release it. According to local press reports, the Treasury Police refused to turn over the vehicle because it contained subversive material.[256]

CGT leader Jose Luis Grande Presa told the Lawyers Committee that the victim took the same route home each day. "It was a well planned assassination. They were waiting for him," he said.[257]

The Investigation

In an attempt to clear up the case, a CGT official met with the Vice Minister of Public Security, the Minister of Defense and the head of the Treasury Police, and during that encounter was himself threatened.[258] Seemingly acknowledging some role in the case, a Treasury Police spokesman was quoted in a *Prensa Grafica* article on May 8, 1988, saying that the force was obligated to clear up the matter.

Justice Minister Julio Samayoa, the chairman of the Commission on Investigations, the parent organ of the Special Investigative Unit (SIU), told the Lawyers Committee in September 1988 that with the assistance of the victim's brother as well as witnesses to his capture, a suspect had been identified. Samayoa

---

[255]Testimony of Rosa Lidia Perdomo, May 10, 1988, Colonia El Pepeto, Soyapango.

[256]*La Prensa Grafica*, May 8, 1988.

[257]Lawyers Committee interview with Jose Grande Presa, July 13, 1988.

[258]Lawyers Committee interviews in San Salvador, July 13, 1988 and January 12, 1989.

said that the Treasury Police had first been implicated because they were in possession of the car, which he said is standard procedure for a vehicle involved in a crime.

Jose Luis Grande Presa said that while his union had cooperated with the SIU he has "no confidence in them. As long as the Treasury Police are involved, they are not going to touch it."[259] He said witnesses had been frightened off when SIU artists had made drawings of them, making them feel like they were under investigation.

Col. Dionisio Machuca, the new director of the Treasury Police, told the Lawyers Committee in September that the union "has tried to politicize the case. The Treasury Police originally investigated the matter and found the car. That's our link to the murder. And we gave the car back to the owner. If we had been responsible we would not have given the car back," Machuca said. He charged the CGT with "pushing confrontation by distributing information" about the death. [260]

In early November 1988, the Special Investigative Unit announced that its six-month investigation had ended in the detention of two suspects, Armando Dominguez Claros and Cesar Augusto Ramirez Grande.[261] Both men were ordered detained in Mariona prison by San Salvador's Fourth Penal Judge. According to the SIU's account, the victim had been involved in a personal dispute with one of the men 10 years ago. During an argument the two exchanged gunshots, leaving one of the men an invalid in a

---

[259]Lawyers Committee interview with Jose Luis Grande Presa, July 13, 1988.

[260]Lawyers Committee interview with Col. Leopoldo Antonio Hernandez, Deputy Vice-Minister of Public Security; Col. Jose Humberto Gomez, Director of the National Guard; Col. Dionisio Machuca, Director of the Treasury Police; Col. Carlos Mauricio Guzman Aguilar, Director of the National Police, September 13, 1988, Estado Mayor. *El Mundo*, May 2, 1988; *La Prensa Grafica*, May 2 and 8, 1988; paid advertisement by CTD, *El Mundo*, May 8, 1988; Tutela Legal. Interview with widow and records of Juez de Paz; *Diario Latino*, May 7, 1988.

[261]*Diario Latino*, November 1 and 4, 1988.

wheelchair. The killing of Adrian Chavarria Giron in April 1988 was then an act of revenge, according to the SIU.

Interviewed in January 1989 in the UNOC offices, human rights secretary Danilo Umana said the union found the SIU version "not credible."[262] Umana said that Chavarria Giron had been killed 300 meters from a Treasury Police roadblock and had already passed two such roadblocks before his detention. Umana added that neighbors he interviewed at 6:00 a.m. the morning after the unionist's murder said they heard shots from the roadblock between 7:00 and 9:00 p.m. the night before.

Umana also told the Lawyers Committee that the union has relocated Chavarria Giron's widow, who has received telephoned threats warning her to be silent about what happened to her husband.

---

[262]Lawyers Committee interview with Danilo Umana, January 12, 1989.

Jose Raul Henriquez
July 29, 1987

The Murder

Three armed members of the Civil Defense of Las Delicias knocked on the door of Jose Raul Henriquez, 38, about 10:00 p.m. on July 29, 1987. Henriquez' common-law wife, Maria Gloria Martinez Campos, 31, the couple's seven children, ages 2-14, his mother and younger brother were also asleep in the house. Maria Gloria Martinez Campos testified that she lit a candle and opened the door, finding her cousin, Jose Reyes Henriquez, his brother, Angel Henriquez, and another civil defense member named Neftali. All were armed and two wore olive green fatigues.

The men said they wanted a drink, and when she said the family had none, they suggested that her husband go with them to find one. The men insisted that Henriquez get dressed; he told his wife that he would not be needing his baseball cap because he was "going to die" (*voy decidido a morir*).[263]

Discovery of the Body

Maria Gloria Martinez Campos went the next morning to the Civil Defense Commander in Tonacatepeque, who promised to help. She also went to the International Committee of the Red Cross, the nongovernmental Human Rights Commission and to National Guard Headquarters.

Eight days later her uncle, Trinidad Campos -- who heads the Civil Defense in the nearby village of Malacoff -- told her that her husband's body was in San Jose Primero. Trinidad Campos, a cattle trader, then threatened the family, telling them he was "authorized to kill them all off."

Too frightened to go by herself, Martinez Campos first went to the remote spot under a tree in Canton San Jose on August 18, 1987, accompanied by the Justice of the Peace of Tonacatepeque, members of the National Association of Agricultural Workers

---

[263]Lawyers Committee interview with Maria Gloria Martinez Campos, January 15, 1988; Investigacion Judicial, Juzgado de Paz de San Martin, August 21, 1987. Tutela Legal, interview with widow, August 21, 1987.

(ANTA), and the nongovernmental Human Rights Commission. The body was identified at 1:45 p.m. by the Justice of the Peace of Tonacatepeque who found that the victim had been killed by a bullet to the head.[264] The body, lying in the open for nearly two months, had been eaten by animals. Henriquez' body was identifiable only by the clothing he had worn at the time of his abduction.

The Possible Motive

A leader of the militant opposition FESTIAVTSCES[265] trade union federation, Jose Raul Henriquez had worked at a poultry farm until it closed. He then began working as an organizer for ANTA, which assists peasant cooperatives in obtaining credit and achieving better wages and conditions for agricultural workers. Because of his work with ANTA, his wife's relatives in the civil defense had accused him of being a guerrilla. His widow also testified that he had been involved in a petty dispute with one of his wife's uncles over a watch.[266]

The Investigation

In her testimony to the Justice of the Peace in San Martin, Maria Gloria Martinez Campos told the story of her husband's detention and named his captors.[267] The names also appeared in an article in San Salvador's daily *El Mundo* on August 19, 1987. After the piece appeared, the three men showed up at the victim's home, asking who had provided their names to the newspaper. Martinez Campos denied having provided their names to the newspaper, but when she was asked, admitted that she had filed a complaint concerning her husband's death with the commander of the Civil Defense in Tonacatepeque. Threatened by the men, she returned to the commander and asked him to erase the complaint, which he did.

---

[264]Reconocimiento Medico, August 18, 1987.

[265]FESTIAVTSCES stands for *Federacion de Sindicatos de Trabajadores de la Industria del Alimento, Vestido, Textil, Similares y Conexos* (Federation of Unions of Workers in the Food, Clothing, Textile and Related Industries).

[266]Lawyers Committee summary of the case, January 1988.

[267]Declaracion de Ofendido, Juzgado 2. de Paz de San Martin, 10:00 a.m. August 20, 1987.

Frightened by this encounter, Maria Gloria Martinez Campos moved to San Salvador with her seven children. Interviewed by the Lawyers Committee in January 1988, Maria Gloria Martinez Campos reiterated her accusations against her two cousins and Neftali.

The SIU suspended its investigation of the case, stating: "The act was supposedly committed by members of the Civil Defense of Tonacatepeque, but there are no eyewitnesses to the crime."[268] The Human Rights Department of the Attorney General's office interviewed the widow. According to Lic. Lazo, however, she said she could not identify the men who took her husband away.[269] Acknowledging that she was probably frightened, Lazo said she had failed to return to give more information when requested to do so.

Interviewed by the Human Rights Institute of the Central American University in December 1988, Martinez Campos said that while she had failed to keep one appointment for lack of transportation, she was willing to cooperate with authorities and could still identify the suspects.

---

[268]*Nomina de casos asignados a la unidad ejecutiva de la comision de investigacion de hechos delictivos.*

[269]Lawyers Committee interview, July 11, 1988, and September 27, 1988, Attorney General's office.

B. ATTACKS ON THE LEGAL AND HUMAN RIGHTS COMMUNITIES

In El Salvador judges and lawyers, particularly those involved in politically sensitive cases, have themselves frequently been targeted for violence. Commenting on this pattern in 1981, the International Commission of Jurists (ICJ) wrote:

> The judiciary has been made impotent by fear, while the magistrates who have attempted to investigate crimes attributed to the security forces or right-wing groups have been immediately attacked, and several of them have been murdered.[270]

One prominent case at that time involved Judge Atilio Ramirez Amaya, the presiding judge in Archbishop Romero's case. On March 26, 1980, there was an assassination attempt against Judge Ramirez Amaya, who then fled the country. The attack was directly linked to his efforts to investigate the murder of the Archbishop. Another example, also reported by the ICJ, involved a judge from San Salvador. According to the ICJ, five relatives of the judge, including two adolescents and a 28-year-old woman, were assassinated on April 14, 1981. The ICJ report adds, "Their heads were severed from their bodies and laid at the doorstep of the judge's home."[271]

On February 23, 1980, the country's Attorney General, Mario Zamora, was killed by masked gunmen who lowered themselves over the roof and down onto the patio of his home, where he was socializing with friends. The murder came a few days after Roberto D'Aubuisson went on television to denounce Zamora and his brother Ruben as guerrillas.[272]

In its 1983 report, *Justice in El Salvador*, the Association of the Bar of the City of New York concluded:

---

[270]International Commission of Jurists, Human Rights in the World: El Salvador, 26 ICJ Review 3, June 1981.

[271]Case Reports: El Salvador, 7 *CIJL Bulletin* 15, p.26, 1981.

[272]Ruben Zamora promptly left the country, but has since returned to lead the Democratic Covergence. See Raymond Bonner, *Weakness and Deceit: U.S. Policy and El Salvador* (Times Books, 1984) pp.102-104.

Intimidation of judges, jurors, prosecutors, witnesses and opposing parties also has long antecedents within the Salvadoran legal system. However, these practices have been greatly aggravated by the recent elevation of violence within the country as a whole. [....] it is in the context of the investigation and prosecution of security force personnel that the impact of judicial intimidation becomes most apparent.[273]

In his February 1989 report to the United Nations, Professor Jose Antonio Pastor Ridruejo, Special Representative on El Salvador, also concluded that "...judges, witnesses and other persons involved in criminal proceedings are not provided with special protection and are exposed to intimidation and coercion, if not to attempts on their lives as happened in the case of Judge Serrano Panameno."[274]

Also targeted for harassment are members of El Salvador's human rights community. On August 14, 1988, four members of Tutela Legal, the human rights office of the Archdiocese of San Salvador, were prohibited by soldiers along the Honduran/Salvadoran border from witnessing the repatriation of Salvadoran refugees from Honduras, and from attending a Church meeting in the area.[275] Two members of the nongovernmental Human Rights Commission of El Salvador were detained for nine hours on February 10, 1988 as they returned from investigating some alleged killings in Chalatenango; another CDHES activist and a visiting U.S. professor were detained last January. The CDHES has been hard-hit over the years; in October 1987 Commission head Herbert Anaya became the fourth member to be killed.

---

[273]"Justice in El Salvador: A Report of a Mission of Inquiry of the Association of the Bar of the City of New York," Adrian De Wind and Stephen Kass, *The Record*, Volume 38, no.2, March 1983, pp. 10 and 11.

[274]"Informe Definitivo", paragraph 75, pp.17-18.

[275]See "The Persecution of Human Rights Monitors, December 1987 to December 1988, A Worldwide Survey," (Human Rights Watch, December 1988) pp.76-79.

Judge Jorge Alberto Serrano Panameno
May 11, 1988

The Killing

Dr. Jorge Alberto Serrano Panameno pulled into his driveway at 7:00 a.m. on May 11, 1988, having just dropped his four children off at school.[276] Serrano had not yet gotten out of his white Hi-Ace Toyota when gunmen pulled up in a car, spraying the 45-year-old military judge with bullets of various calibre. A postmortem examination conducted by Dr. Juan Mateu Llort revealed seven bullet wounds in the chest and throat; two bullets were extracted from the body for examination by the U.S.-funded Special Investigative Unit.[277]

The Possible Motive

Serrano, a civilian, had served three years as First Military Judge of First Instance and was responsible for two politically

---

[276]This account is based on the following sources: *Washington Post*, May 12, 1988; *La Prensa Grafica*, May 17, 1988; Tutela Legal, Recopilacion de datos de la investigacion judicial, segun Juzgado Cuarto de Paz de San Salvador, May 11, 1988; Acta de Reconocimiento by Juez Cuarto de Paz, Lic. Rafael Arsenio Iglesias Cortez, May 11, 1988; Reconocimiento by Dr. Juan Mateu Llort, May 11, 1988; and other court documents reviewed by the Lawyers Committee, July 13, 1988; *El Mundo*, May 12, 1988; *Diario de Hoy*, May 16 and 19, 1988; *La Prensa Grafica*, May 13, 1988; *Christian Science Monitor*, May 12, 1988; *The New York Times*, May 12, 1988.

[277]"Reconocimiento", May 11, 1988, By Dr. Juan Mateu Llort at the Centro Judicial Isidro Menendez.

controversial cases[278] at the time of his death, both initiated under State of Emergency Decree 50 procedures.[279]

Judge Serrano was killed just days before he was expected to rule on an amnesty petition filed by defense attorneys for three men jailed since April 1986 in a kidnapping-for-profit case.

Implicated in the kidnapping ring were several rightist military officers who held at least five wealthy conservative businessmen for ransom between March 1982 and February 1986. In a 16-page confession, one of the suspects, Rodolfo Isidro Lopez Sibrian, said that the kidnapping ring's activities netted more than $1.25 million,[280] though *The Washington Post* placed the figure as high as $4 million.[281] The officers, who posed as left-wing guerrillas, are all close associates of Roberto D'Aubuisson, who has not been formally accused of participation in the ring.[282] In a two-part expose on death squads published in August 1988, *The Washington Post* reported that "With money growing short and their power waning, [death squad members] turned to kidnapping wealthy

---

[278]In November 1987, Serrano granted amnesty to three suspected leftist rebels accused of killing 13 people in a San Salvador sidewalk cafe in June 1985. Among those killed in the Zona Rosa entertainment district were four U.S. Marine guards attached to the U.S. Embassy and two U.S. civilians, both employees of the Wang computer company. That ruling was upheld by a higher military court in late January 1988. Threatened with the loss of $18.5 million in U.S. aid if the three were freed, President Jose Napoleon Duarte -- as last instance of appeal in the military justice system -- overturned the ruling in April 1988. The three remain jailed in San Miguel, San Vicente and Santa Ana pending trial.

[279]Decree 50 was the law regulating detention and sentencing procedures during a State of Exception, which existed in El Salvador from March 1980 until January 1987, when it lapsed on its own terms. Under Decree 50, civilians implicated in certain crimes were tried by a military tribunal. Those suspected of affiliation with the FMLN were brought before the military courts.

[280]Jefferson Morley, "Salvador Justice: The Curious Case of Colonel Staben," *The New Republic*, September 8, 1986.

[281]*Washington Post*, May 11, 1988.

[282]*Washington Post*, May 11, 1988.

127

businessmen to maintain their lifestyles, making it appear to be the work of leftist rebels...."[283]

The three men incarcerated between 1986 and 1989 in the kidnapping case were: cashiered Lieutenant Rodolfo Isidro Lopez Sibrian; his father-in-law, Luis Orlando Llovera Ballete, a wealthy landowner; and Maj. Jose Alfredo Jimenez. Lopez Sibrian was implicated in the 1981 killings of Jose Rodolfo Viera, a land reform official, and two U.S. advisors, Michael Hammer and Mark David Pearlman.[284] According to several testimonies in that case, he was the intellectual author of the "Sheraton murders." Despite extensive proof linking him to those murders, the Salvadoran Supreme Court ordered a "definite stay of proceedings" against Lopez Sibrian in November 1984.[285]

Other suspects in the ransom ring have been associated with government Security Forces and death squads. Three men detained in connection with the case died while in custody. Ramon Erasmo Oporto Terezon, brother-in-law of Lopez Sibrian and a former National Police detective, was found hanged in his cell two days after his detention;[286] another was former National Police detective Edgar Perez Linares, who was believed to have directed the Secret Anticommunist Army death squad. By at least one account, Linares -- who was a protege of Roberto D'Aubuisson -- is reported to have gunned down Archbishop Oscar Arnulfo Romero in 1980.[287] Linares died in May 1986 when he allegedly attempted to escape from custody of the Salvadoran National Police, who were bringing him in for questioning. A third suspect, Moises Lopez Arriola, died in a shoot-out with authorities[288]. Three other suspects -- Victor Antonio Cornejo Arango, Lt. Joaquin Zacapa, and Lt. Carlos

---

[283]*Washington Post*, August 29, 1988.

[284]See p.29 for a discussion of the Sheraton case.

[285]See *El Salvador: Human Rights Dismissed, A Report on 16 Unresolved Cases* (Lawyers Committee for Human Rights, 1986) pp.17-27.

[286]*Miami Herald*, April 6, 1986.

[287]*Washington Post*, August 29, 1988.

[288]*The Civilian Toll, 1986-1987* (Americas Watch, 9th supplement, August 30, 1987), p.240.

Zacapa, all linked to death squads, have fled the country. Salvadoran investigators told foreign journalists that they suspect that the men were killed to keep them from talking.[289]

The home of Judge Miriam Artiaga, who handled another part of the case, was machine-gunned twice in March 1987. Judge Artiaga resigned and in August 1987, Carlos Roberto Urbina was named to replace her as Judge of First Instance in Apopa.[290]

Defense attorneys sought to dismiss the case despite the fact that El Salvador's amnesty law specifically exempts kidnapping and extortion cases. In a statement televised the day before his murder, Judge Serrano said that amnesty was not appropriate but he indicated that he would apply the amnesty to pending charges for illegal possession of weapons, an action that would have deprived his court of jurisdiction in the case. If this action were taken, the remaining charges would have been sent to a civilian criminal court. It was widely reported that Judge Serrano was under considerable pressure to grant amnesty in this case and that he had turned down a number of attempted bribes.[291]

Uncovering the Kidnapping Ring

On numerous occasions in recent years senior officials at the U.S. Embassy in San Salvador have singled out the kidnapping-for-profit investigation as a test case for the Salvadoran justice system. At an early stage in the proceedings, both the FBI and the Special Investigative Unit (SIU) were said to have been

---

[289]*Washington Post*, May 22, 1988.

[290]*Washington Post*, May 12, 1988 and Lawyers Committee interview with Judge Urbina, Tonacatepeque, May 18, 1988. The kidnapping ring is also charged with the theft of a metal structure. The men dismantled and removed the superstructure of a building as it was being built. UPI reported on April 23, 1987 that Llovera confessed to hiring 50 men to steal the structure. See also *The Civilian Toll, 1986-1987* (Americas Watch, 9th supplement, August 30, 1987) pp. 237-244.

[291]*Christian Science Monitor*, May 12, 1988; Summary prepared for the Lawyers Committee, May 11, 1988; *Washington Post*, April 3, 1989.

aiding the search,[292] but a list of SIU cases provided to the Lawyers Committee in July 1988 does not include the kidnapping case.[293]

In late 1985, an informal investigating committee of business and government representatives -- headed by then vice-minister for public security, Col. Reynaldo Lopez Nuila -- was formed in response to pressure from the victims' families, who also hired their own investigator.[294] The work of the group led to the first detention of suspects in late March 1986 and the discovery of clandestine basement cells where the men were held.

A U.S. Embassy official told the Lawyers Committee that money from the Administration of Justice Program had been used to purchase a partition for Judge Serrano's office, a locked safe to store sensitive documents and various other items out of "petty cash," and to pay the salary of his administrative assistant.[295] U.S. AID officials in the Office of Democratic Initiatives said the judge had not requested and therefore did not receive personal protection.[296]

Investigation of Serrano's Murder

Justice Minister Julio Alfredo Samayoa told the Lawyers Committee in July that evidence uncovered in the SIU investigation implicated the kidnapping ring in Serrano's murder and that suspects had been identified among the defense attorneys. But interviewed in early September, Samayoa reported that the investigation had sharply changed course. Ballistic evidence analyzed by the Forensic Laboratory of the Special Investigative Unit had linked bullets from

---

[292]Summary of the kidnapping case prepared for the Lawyers Committee, April 28, 1986.

[293]"Nomina de Casos...," provided by Justice Minister Samayoa, July 15, 1988. Judge Serrano's death is, however, listed among the SIU's active cases.

[294]Jefferson Morley, "Salvador Justice: The Curious Case of Colonel Staben," *The New Republic*, September 8, 1986.

[295]Lawyers Committee interview, U.S. Embassy, San Salvador, May 20, 1988.

[296]Interview with staff of the Office of Democratic Initiatives, AID, San Salvador, May 23, 1988.

two of the murder weapons to three other unsolved murders. In at least one of these cases, Salvadoran officials had in the past suggested that blame lay with the FMLN. Samayoa said a suspect was under surveillance and arrest was imminent. Though court files reviewed by the Lawyers Committee mention no eyewitnesses to the murder, Justice Minister Samayoa said statements have been taken from three witnesses who will be called in to identify the suspect.

In September, Attorney General Roberto Giron Flores told the Lawyers Committee that his department had not investigated the judge's death since it "did not have the capacity to do so." In a separate interview on September 27, Lic. Arturo Lazo, in charge of human rights cases in the Attorney General's office, said he was awaiting completion of the work of the Special Investigative Unit before deciding whether to prosecute the case.

Supreme Court President Dr. Francisco Guerrero said the SIU had not briefed him on its five-month-old investigation. "They say they know who did it but they don't tell us. It must be too politically sensitive," he told the Lawyers Committee, arguing that as "the head of the judicial family" the court had a right to expect a confidential briefing.[297]

Court files examined on April 3, 1989 revealed that the Attorney General's office petitioned the judge repeatedly to request information on the case from the SIU and the Security Forces. Only when it was presented for the third time, on February 11, 1989, was the petition granted.[298]

On May 11 the State Department said Serrano was among El Salvador's "real heroes" who had "courageously carried out his work in the face of pressure from the left and the right" and pledged to assist in the investigation.[299] A statement prepared for the noon press briefing in Washington read:

---

[297]Lawyers Committee interview with Dr. Francisco Jose Guerrero, Supreme Court, San Salvador, September 14, 1988.

[298]The court files were reviewed by IDHUCA on April 3, 1989.

[299]UPI, May 11, 1988 as cited in *La Prensa Grafica*, May 13, 1988.

The assassination of Judge Serrano is a setback to the cause of implementing a functioning judicial system in El Salvador. A murder like this can not but cause judges to think twice when they render decisions in sensitive cases. Judge Serrano was a patriot and a dedicated professional who took on sensitive cases and administered justice not according to political or pecuniary motivations but according to the law. He was one of the heroes responsible for furthering the democratic process and the rule of law in El Salvador.

In a strongly worded denunciation of the "cowardly assassination" of Serrano, the Duarte Administration called on the "citizenry to help in clearing up this perfidious assassination and in stopping the spiral of violence and terrorism devastating our country." Affirming the government's intention to get to the bottom of the matter, the statement also mentioned the "increase in irrational terrorism in the last two months."[300]

The Aftermath

On August 16, 1988, the Supreme Court named Second Military Judge of First Instance, Dr. Jorge Ernesto Cruz Cienfuegos, to replace Serrano. In late 1988, Dr. Cruz Cienfuegos amnestied the illegal possession of firearms portion of the kidnapping-for-profit case, declared himself "incompetent," and referred the matter to Juan Hector Larios Larios, San Salvador's Third Penal Judge. According to Article 3, paragraph 3 of El Salvador's amnesty law, kidnapping is excluded from the list of crimes for which amnesty may be granted. Illegal possession of firearms was the only charge that fell within amnesty provisions.[301]

Charges Dismissed and Quickly Reinstated

On March 31, Judge Juan Hector Larios Larios dismissed all charges in the kidnapping case, just 20 minutes before his tenure

---

[300]SISAL, May 12, 1988 as cited in *El Mundo*, May 12, 1988.

[301]A U.S. Embassy official told the Lawyers Committee on January 19, 1989 that the exact charges in the kidnapping case have never been clear. "There are two different documents with two different versions," the official said.

ended at San Salvador's Third Penal Court. He ordered that all three suspects be released immediately.[302] Orlando Llovera made it to the Guatemalan border, where he was stopped; Maj. Jose Alfredo Jimenez, still on active duty, returned to his barracks. Lopez Sibrian was not immediately freed, pending the completion of paperwork.

On April 3, the National Association of Private Enterprise (ANEP) took out a paid advertisement in *La Prensa Grafica* "condemning the release of the kidnappers." According to an article in *Diario de Hoy* the same day, ANEP said Larios' ruling had caused "true moral and juridical chaos in the judicial field." *Diario Latino* quoted President Duarte and an unnamed "high-ranking ARENA leader" emphatically criticising dismissal of the case.

That same day, Supreme Court President Guerrero suspended Judge Larios from his new post at Santa Ana's Third Civil Court and prohibited him from practicing law, pending outcome of an inquiry. Larios' replacement at San Salvador's Third Penal Court, Dr. Ricardo Mejia Angulo, examined the evidence and reversed the earlier ruling.

Maj. Jimenez and Rodolfo Isidro Lopez Sibrian remain in custody; Orlando Llovera, brought back to San Salvador where he was held in house arrest, slipped away and his whereabouts are unknown.

Reached by telephone on April 3, the Justice Minister said the investigation of Serrano's death "is still pending and investigators have recently turned up a new thread. It's difficult to say who killed Judge Serrano. In this country, it could be anybody."

---

[302]*Washington Post*, April 3, 1989; *New York Times*, April 3, 1989.

Herbert Ernesto Anaya Sanabria
October 26, 1987

The Killing

Herbert Ernesto Anaya Sanabria, coordinator of the nongovernmental Human Rights Commission of El Salvador (CDHES), was murdered at about 6:35 a.m. on October 26, 1987. He was shot in a parking lot near his brick row house in the Jose Simeon Canas neighborhood of Zacamil, San Salvador. Mr. Anaya, 33, had left the house ahead of his wife and children to warm up the car in preparation for taking them to school. Ten-year-old Rosa Margarita and her younger sister were the first to reach the scene and sounded the alarm to their mother, 32-year-old Mirna Perla de Anaya. Mrs. Anaya, a law professor and former judge in Suchitoto, told the press that she did not hear the shooting, and that her husband of 10 years was dead by the time she reached him.[303]

---

[303]*Los Angeles Times*, November 17, 1987. By all accounts, the gunmen used silencers. On October 28, 1987, *The New York Times* cited "Western diplomats" who said they had concluded that the gunmen "were members of a right-wing death squad, the only kind of group known to use weapons as sophisticated as silencers."

The judicial recognition of the body was conducted by the Seventh Justice of the Peace of San Salvador, Lic. Vilma Adela Melara, at 8:30 a.m. at the Isidro Menendez Judicial Center. A forensic doctor who examined the body found four lesions caused by firearms, apparently 9 mm. calibre; two bullets were extracted for examination and were turned over to Justice Vilma Adela Melara. "Informe Preliminar Sobre la Muerte de Herbert Ernesto Anaya Sanabria," Tutela Legal. Tutela employees were present during the "recognition."

According to an account published in *El Diario de Hoy* on October 30, 1987, Dr. Perla de Anaya gave her statement to the Justice on October 29 saying that neighbors told her that two men, one quite young, had shot her husband using silencers, wrapping the weapons afterward in a blue jacket; a third man provided protection. The three escaped in a pick-up with polarized windows which had been parked about 50 meters away.

134

Herbert Anaya was a co-founder of the CDHES and had worked with the organization since 1980.[304] He was the fourth Commission member to be killed; three others have disappeared. On March 16, 1983, Commission President Marianela Garcia Villas, who, fearing for her life, had moved to Mexico, was murdered during a fact-finding mission to El Salvador.[305] A CDHES spokesman said another member, Maria Victoria Hernandez Gonzalez, was abducted by the National Police on October 11, 1987 and during "interrogations and threats" was told that "the actions against our organization would continue and that they were going to discredit all the work we have done."[306] According to other accounts, Hernandez Gonzalez was warned that Herbert Anaya would be "dealt with."[307] Anaya's father, Rafael Anaya Garcia, was arrested by soldiers on March 4, 1987 and questioned for two days about his son's human rights work, before being released.[308]

Mr. Anaya was previously arrested on the evening of May 26, 1986 following public accusations by a former Commission member that Anaya was an FMLN militant.[309] According to the

---

[304]The Human Rights Commission is one of six non-governmental rights monitoring organizations in El Salvador: Tutela Legal, the human rights office of the Archdiocese of San Salvador; Socorro Juridico Cristiano, Arzobispo Oscar Romero; Instituto de Derechos Humanos de la Universidad Centroamericana, Jose Simeon Canas (IDHUCA); the human rights department of the Union Nacional Obrero Campesino (UNOC); and the human rights department of the Lutheran Church.

[305]*Third Supplement to the Report on Human Rights in El Salvador*, (Americas Watch/The American Civil Liberties Union, July 19, 1983), pp.32-36.

[306]Radio Cadena YSU, San Salvador, October 26, 1987, cited in FBIS-LAT-87-207, October 27, 1987.

[307]National Public Radio, October 26, 1987; Amnesty International newsletter, Vol.17, no.12, p.8, December 1987.

[308]*CIJL Bulletin*, Geneva, April 1988.

[309]See for example, *Los Angeles Times*, November 17, 1987. Seven other members of human rights organizations were also arrested as a result of the accusations. Some of them were severely tortured while in custody; all were eventually released without

Los Angeles Times, Mr. Anaya was en route to buy soft drinks with his wife and three youngest children when he was snatched from the street by "two men in tennis shoes and jeans [who] emerged from a blue pick-up with opaque windows. They threw Herbert Anaya up against the truck and struck him with the butts of their guns before pushing him inside."[310]

During his imprisonment Anaya Sanabria and other jailed CDHES members interviewed fellow political detainees about their treatment while in custody. Their extensive findings on torture were detailed in a report which was smuggled out of Mariona.[311]

He was let out of jail in February 1987 when the government agreed to exchange 53 political detainees in Mariona's La Esperanza prison for the release of Air Force Col. Omar Napoleon Avalos, held by the FMLN since October 1985.

The Public Reaction

The killing of Herbert Anaya was widely condemned in El Salvador and abroad. A survey of Salvadoran newspapers in the days following the murder turns up denunciations in the form of paid advertisements,[312] press releases and articles from a range of groups, domestic and foreign, among them: U.S. trade unions, academic, artistic, and religious leaders; the rest of the country's human rights community -- including ASPRODERH and the

---

charges. The former CDHES member who raised the charges later founded another human rights group, the Salvadoran Association for Human Rights (ASPRODERH).

[310]*Los Angeles Times*, November 17, 1987.

[311]"La Tortura en El Salvador," September 24, 1986, Comision de Derechos Humanos de El Salvador (CDHES). An English edition was released by the Marin Interfaith Task Force on Central America under the title, "Torture in El Salvador" October 1986.

[312]Given right-wing control of most of the media, *campos pagados*, or paid ads, are a common means of publicity in El Salvador, particularly by opposition groups.

136

governmental CDH[313]; Salvadoran opposition trade unions and political parties; the Danish and Swedish sections of Amnesty International; and the Ministry of Culture and Communications. According to *El Mundo*, the Mexican Chamber of Deputies unanimously adopted a resolution of "energetic condemnation"; UN Secretary-General Javier Perez de Cuellar released a statement deploring "all violent acts of this nature"; and Christian Democratic Foreign Minister Hans Dietrich Genscher of the Federal Republic of Germany expressed indignation at the "cowardly assassination" of Anaya.[314] U.S. Ambassador Edwin Corr called the killing "an aberration" committed by "four fanatic cats who have nothing to do with the government of El Salvador or the Armed Forces."[315]

Domestic opposition groups demonstrated for five days in San Salvador -- including an all-night vigil outside the U.S. Embassy -- culminating their activities with Anaya Sanabria's funeral on October 30, 1987. In protest, the FMLN called a traffic stoppage on November 3 and on October 29 announced they would not attend peace talks with the government scheduled for that week in Mexico City.[316]&[317]

---

[313]The governmental CDH placed an ad in *La Prensa Grafica* on October 27 "manifesting...its total and complete repudiation of this criminal act" and went on to "express...its solidarity with the CDHES...." On October 28 *La Prensa Grafica* reported that the CDH had invited the Inter-American Commission on Human Rights of the OAS to visit El Salvador in order to "confirm and give testimony to the exhaustive investigations" into Anaya's murder.

[314]SALPRES-NOTISAL, October 29, 1987; *El Mundo*, October 29, 1987.

[315]*El Diario de Hoy*, October 28, 1987.

[316]In a communique read on the clandestine Radio Venceremos on October 30 the FMLN said the decision should be viewed "as a gesture of condemnation of the crime committed by the government and the Armed Forces of El Salvador. To attend this meeting would contribute to creating false expectations and distract national and international attention." See also *New York Times*, October 30, 1987; *El Mundo*, October 30, 1987.

[317]Dr. Mario Reni Roldan, head of the Social Democratic Party, resigned from the National Reconciliation Commission -- appointed to monitor El Salvador's compliance with the Esquipulas peace

Government critics among the nongovernmental community suggested responsibility for the death lay with right-wing death squads or with the Armed Forces. Msgr. Rivera y Damas condemned the killing in his November 1 homily and cited Tutela Legal's report which "attributed [the act] to the death squads."[318]

In its October 26 press conference the CDHES charged:

that complete responsibility for this murder falls on the Armed Forces High Command, the security corps, and the government itself. This is not a new or strange action. The Armed Forces and the High Command have carried out numerous actions since our organization was founded many years ago.[319]

The Armed Forces, rejecting what it called "irresponsible declarations by individuals belonging to the self-styled nongovernmental Human Rights Commission and other mass organizations" reminded the public in a paid advertisement on October 26, 1987 of its exemplary behavior during the early October

---

process -- "due to the incapacity of the government to impede the escalation of violations of human rights." Citing the death of Herbert Anaya and another opposition leader, Roldan said "This situation discredits the government version that it is in compliance with the agreements of Esquipulas II...." *El Mundo*, October 28, 1987, as cited in El Rescate Chronology, October 1987.

[318]*El Mundo*, November 2, 1987.

[319]San Salvador Radio Cadena YSU, October 26, 1987 as cited in FBIS-LAT-87-207, October 27, 1987, p.11. "The Third Supplement to the Report on Human Rights in El Salvador" published by Americas Watch and the American Civil Liberties Union on July 19, 1983 details attacks on the Commission during its earliest years. Among the abuses is the February 1983 disappearance of a founding member of the CDHES, a physician who treated the victims of human rights violations, and the September 1980 bombing of the Commission's offices (see Third Supplement, pp. 32-36).

visit of two exiled opposition leaders[320]. Denying culpability in the death, the military asked the public not to be taken in by "tendentious declarations which hide the strategic plans of national and international subversion."[321]

Within days representatives of the country's Christian Democratic government began to "accuse the extreme left of responsibility for the crime, as a strategy to confuse public opinion at home and abroad," according to *La Prensa Grafica*, which cited statements made to the media by President Duarte and Defense Minister Eugenio Vides Casanova.[322] Asserting that "The death squads have been disbanded," then Deputy Minister of Culture and Communication Roberto Edmundo Viera did not rule out that rightists could have killed Anaya, but said:

> If we compare the terrorists actions that we have been facing, most of them have not been staged by the death squads but by the FMLN structures.[323]

The Investigation

President Duarte offered a 50,000 *colones* ($10,000) reward to anyone providing information leading to identification of the assassins[324] and officials announced that investigations had been launched by the Commission on Investigations and the Security Forces.[325] The Amnesty law, approved by the Assembly on October 28, was back-dated to exclude the Anaya murder.

---

[320]A dialogue between the government and the opposition was held on October 4-6, 1987 in San Salvador with the mediation of San Salvador's Archbishop and Auxiliary Bishop. Several FMLN commanders came down from the hills for the talks; Ruben Zamora and Guillermo Ungo, who were still living abroad at the time, returned to El Salvador for the meeting.

[321]*La Prensa Grafica*, October 27, 1987.

[322]*La Prensa Grafica*, October 31, 1987.

[323]San Salvador Television Nacional, October 27, 1987, as cited in FBIS-LAT-87-208, October 28, 1987, p.3.

[324]*El Diario de Hoy*, October 29, 1987.`

[325]*El Mundo*, October 26, 1987.

On October 29 detectives from the National Police's Technical Laboratory announced they had elaborated sketches of the two gunmen based on the descriptions of an unnamed eyewitness.[326] The U.S.-funded Commission on Investigations placed an advertisement in the press seeking the cooperation of the public and provided a telephone number where information could be shared anonymously.[327]

On November 3 a self-described eyewitness appeared before the Seventh Justice of the Peace asserting that the crime was committed by members of the Vindictive Antiterrorist Commando *Los Magnificos*.[328] Again going public with its investigation, the Commission on Investigations placed a communique in at least two San Salvador dailies detailing the results of their investigation of witness Jose Luis Hernandez Lima, whom they concluded had fabricated the story to collect the 50,000 *colones* reward.[329]

The Commission also "implored" the Anaya family to provide any detail that could help clear up the crime, and reminded the citizenry of the reward.

Anaya Sanabria's widow, Mirna Perla de Anaya, told the Justice of the Peace in late October that her house as well as the CDHES offices were constantly surveilled by unknown men.[330] In November she told the Lawyers Committee that because of the surveillance her children were panic-stricken and that she planned to leave the country.[331] Two detectives from the SIU arrived at her home, forcing the maid to let them in. Dr. Perla de Anaya later learned from relatives that the SIU had sought information from them about her, including whether she had a boyfriend.

---

[326]*Diario de Hoy*, October 29, 1987.

[327]*El Mundo*, October 30, 1987.

[328]*La Prensa Grafica*, November 4, 1987; *El Mundo*, November 20, 1987.

[329]*Diario Latino* and *La Prensa Grafica*, November 20, 1987.

[330]*El Diario de Hoy*, October 30, 1987.

[331]Lawyers Committee interview with Mirna Anaya, November 17, 1987.

A Suspect: Jorge Alberto Miranda Arevalo

Days before the International Verification and Follow-Up Commission was to arrive in San Salvador to monitor the country's compliance with the Esquipulas II peace agreement, President Duarte and Justice Minister Julio Samayoa held a press conference to announce that the crime had been solved. Duarte declared, "...we know the truth. We have the moral and police truth."[332] Justice Minister Samayoa, who heads the Commission on Investigations which conducted the search, added, "There is no doubt that a leftist terrorist group killed him."

Jorge Alberto Miranda Arevalo, 19, was arrested on December 23, 1987 as he reportedly attempted to flatten the tires of a Pepsi-Cola delivery truck in Zacamil. A government press release said that "under interrogation" Miranda voluntarily confessed membership in the People's Revolutionary Army (ERP) and when questioned about several recent killings, including that of Herbert Anaya, spontaneously admitted his participation as look-out for the trigger man. The government asserted that Anaya, who they allege also belonged to the ERP, was considered "burned" (*quemado*), no longer useful to the left, and had been passing information to the Armed Forces.[333] The release said that all the details provided by Miranda had been verified and that a polygraph examination had shown him to be truthful.

Miranda Arevalo was held in incommunicado detention for 12 days before his arraignment on January 4, 1988 in violation of Salvadoran law which provides that suspects may be held for no

---

[332]San Salvador Canal 12, January 6, 1988 as cited in FBIS-LAT-88-007, January 12, 1988, p.11.

[333]Government Press Release, January 4, 1988, appearing in *Diario Latino*, January 5, 1988, as cited in FBIS-LAT-88-007, January 12, 1988, p.10. President Duarte added that "it's a clear act of execution by an extremist organization against a person who no longer serves them." He said the killing was designed not only to get rid of someone who no longer did the left's bidding, but to cast the Armed Forces in a negative light, *El Mundo*, January 6, 1988. See also, Declaracion Indagatoria, filed in the First Penal Court, San Salvador, January 4, 1988, 11:45 a.m.

longer than 72 hours without appearing before a judge.[334] The International Committee of the Red Cross (ICRC) was not permitted to visit him during those 12 days.[335]

The Justice Minister said the delay was because the court was on vacation;[336] President Duarte's explanation for the delay turned on the fact that the suspect was picked up for one crime -- sabotage of a Pepsi truck -- and then accused of a second crime -- murder -- and therefore a second 72-hour period was warranted, leaving six days unexplained[337]; and the judge assigned the case, Lic. Luis Edgar Morales Joya, said the violation would not lead to dismissal of the proceedings. "It is common that prisoners are detained longer than the stipulated time."[338] In his appearance before Judge Morales, Miranda ratified his extrajudicial confession, and again admitted his participation in the murder of Herbert Anaya.

Countervailing Testimony

According to the suspect's mother, 49-year-old Otilia Arevalo, the National Police searched the family home on December 27, taking away "as evidence" an appointment calendar and a picture of Archbishop Romero, saying it was "bad" for the family that it had been found.[339] They returned on December 30, this time with Jorge Alberto Miranda in tow. Otilia Arevalo told the Lawyers Committee that her son, who was thin and distraught, cried as he

---

[334]Article 143 of the Criminal Procedure Code reads in part: "Auxiliary organs which detain someone presumed guilty of any type of crime should turn him over to the appropriate judge within 72 hours of the detention...."

[335]Under an agreement with the Salvadoran government, the ICRC is permitted access to detainees after the first three days. See *Washington Post*, January 8, 1988.

[336]FBIS-LAT-88-007, January 12, 1988, p.11.

[337]*El Diario de Hoy*, January 6, 1988.

[338]*El Mundo*, January 11, 1988.

[339]Amnesty International, "El Salvador: Investigation Into Killing of Herbert Anaya: New Developments," February 1988, AMR/29/07/88, p.4.

pointed to a corner of the house where weapons were allegedly buried; the police dug and found nothing.[340] She and her husband saw him again on January 2 for about five minutes; in police custody, the boy cried, saying nothing. On January 3 she talked with him for some six minutes. "In a low voice he said, 'The only thing I want to tell you is that I'm not sleeping because they interrogate me day and night....They want me to collaborate with them,'" she testified.[341]

The couple was summoned by armed men in civilian clothing to appear at National Police headquarters, from where they were driven to the court for their son's arraignment. Held out of earshot at the courts, Otilia Arevalo was approached by a man in a suit who attempted to give her 12,000 colones ($2,400) because "your son is collaborating with us." When she refused the money, the man said it was payment for information on weapons caches that her son had provided.[342]

Learning of the accusations against the youth, the family went public with its own account of events. Interviewed by the Lawyers Committee on January 15, 1988, Miranda's mother and 22-year-old sister, Ana Gladys Miranda Arevalo, a student at the Jesuit University, said Jorge Alberto went to bed at midnight on October 25, staying up later than usual to prepare for a final social studies exam. His mother said he was asleep in bed at 8:30 the next morning when she left for her job as a domestic. His sister Ines, a fellow student in the afternoon shift at the Manuel Jose Arce Institute, says he got up at 9:00 a.m., exercised, bathed, put on his school uniform, and left for school after eating the breakfast she prepared him. Jorge was thus, the family says, in bed asleep when Anaya was killed at 6:35 a.m.[343]

---

[340]Lawyers Committee interview with Otilia Arevalo and Ana Gladys Miranda Arevalo, January 15, 1988.

[341]Tutela Legal, January 5, 1988, #02005.

[342]*Ibid.*

[343]In January 1989, Amnesty International issued a summary of developments in the case which reported that "the school where [Miranda] was studying has made documents available, including attendance records and the actual exam taken, which appear to support Jorge Miranda's assertion that on the day of the murder he had been sitting exams." "El Salvador: Continued Detention Without

143

A Publicity Campaign

Miranda's judicial confession was filed in San Salvador's First Penal Court on January 4, 1988. He said he had belonged to the ERP since October 1986 and received weapons training on the Guazapa volcano that November. Known in his guerrilla cell as "Erick," Miranda Arevalo said he participated until his December 1987 capture in acts of sabotage. According to his account, the head of his cell received an order from his superior that Anaya was to be assassinated "because he was not doing a good job as CDHES coordinator. Anaya Sanabria was no longer useful, he was already burned...and had been passing information to the Armed Forces."[344]

Miranda named two other accomplices to the murder; when "Carlos," stationed about three meters from Anaya, opened fire, Miranda said he "heard the shot as though it was 'an exploding rocket' [quotations in the original]; it was about four or six shots that he heard."[345]

Salvadoran officials released daily information on the case, mostly in the press. Miranda's filmed confession appeared on television and a complete transcript of his statement was published in *El Mundo* on January 11 under large block letters *LA VERDAD, BASE DE LA JUSTICIA* [The Truth, the Basis of Justice]. The Ministry of Culture and Communications, which placed the ad, used the same banner headlines several times over the next week: photos showed Miranda at the crime scene re-enacting the events; statements of an unnamed witness were compared with Miranda's, allegedly proving the veracity of Miranda's version; a photo of Miranda and sketches of his accomplices ("ERP Members Accused

---

Trial of Jorge Miranda Arevalo," Amnesty International, January 1989. (AMR 29/04/89).

[344]Declaracion Indagatoria, el Juzgado Primero de lo Penal, San Salvador, 11:45 a.m., January 4, 1988.

[345]Accounts at the time of the killing uniformly say the gunmen used silencers. Miranda's defense attorneys have prepared a document outlining the inconsistencies in the government's case. See *Algunas Incongruencias de la Confesion de Jorge Alberto Miranda Arevalo, Valoraciones de la Defensa*, March 10, 1988.

144

in the Assassination") are juxtaposed with graffiti calling for "Justice and Punishment for the Murderers of Anaya Sanabria."[346]

The conspiracy was given an international angle: a *contra* spokesman announced in San Salvador that the assassination "was planned in Managua by the Sandinistas and executed by the FMLN."[347] On *Radio Venceremos'* January 5 evening broadcast, the FMLN General Command said the guerrilla movement had not murdered the CDHES leader.[348]

In mid-February the government press office released information from alleged guerrilla documents saying that Herbert Anaya had been criticized within the ERP for "opportunism in the management of funds," and being a "womanizer."[349]

The Retraction

From isolation at Mariona prison on February 1, 1988, 19-year-old Miranda submitted a hand-written retraction to his January confession. He explained that he "took responsibility for the events concerning the death because he felt badly and very sick because of how I was treated in the National Police in Zacamil."[350] Miranda writes that "while I was blindfolded they gave me an injection, saying it was for my tonsils. I found this strange, since I'd never had tonsilitis. This and other actions taken against me and my family pressured me into taking responsibility for actions I did not commit."

---

[346]See *El Mundo*, January 9, 11, 13, & 14, 1988; *La Prensa Grafica*, January 13, 1988.

[347]*Diario de Hoy*, January 9, 1988.

[348]*El Mundo*, January 6, 1988. See also Radio Venceremos, January 6, 1988.

[349]*Diario de Hoy*, February 15, 1988; *La Prensa Grafica*, February 16, 1988.

[350]Cited from Miranda's hand-written statement, which was notarized. See also *The Washington Post*, February 19, 1988.

On February 12, the prisoner sent out another note: he wrote that a lieutenant in the National Police and two Venezuelan journalists[351] came to his cell at 11:00 p.m. on February 10 and stayed until 1:20 a.m., questioning him about whether he had voluntarily changed his testimony. They said his attorneys and his mother "were only attempting to destroy me...my mother was playing with the law, that the declaration made by my mother and my sister could land them in jail."[352] They said they "had possibilities to help me get out soon...."

On February 11 the same lieutenant and a National Police agent came and addressed him "in a threatening manner, not giving me a chance to talk...[saying] that I had to make my own independent decisions...." Miranda later told the court that they threatened to transfer him to the section of Mariona for common prisoners if he changed his story.

Though the prisoner had not yet been brought before the judge to give his new statement, the press learned of his intent to file a retraction. On February 19, *The Washington Post* reported that

> the prosecution filed a motion to block him from appearing. Prosecutor Luis Roberto Pineda said the move by Miranda and his lawyers was a tactic designed to confuse public opinion, and that only the

---

[351]Miranda mentioned visits by two Venezuelan journalists several times thoughout his various oral and written statements. Venezuela, like the United States, provides police trainers to the Salvadoran security forces. In his second judicial statement, Miranda testified that "the persons identified as Venezuelan journalists, who had given him a radio and a television, visited him and said they would take them away if he changed his declaration, which they did on Tuesday of this week[February 16, 1988]."
In the same declaration Miranda says a journalist who identified herself as "Ivonne" showed up at 7:30 a.m. on February 18 "asking for an interview in a persistent fashion," which he declined. [Declaracion Indagatoria, Centro Penal "La Esperanza," 9:20 a.m., February 20, 1988.]
Miranda told a reporter for the *Los Angeles Times* that he had related "his story to an unidentified American as well as to National Police interrogators." *Los Angeles Times*, January 9, 1988.

[352] Cited from Miranda's February 10, 1988 statement written in Mariona.

initial judicial confession was valid in court, not amended versions.

The new statement was finally recorded by First Penal Judge Luis Edgar Morales Joya on February 20, 1988 at 9:20 a.m. at the prison. The Mariona director said he had failed to deliver Miranda to give his statement earlier "because he did not have access to a vehicle in which to transport the prisoner," according to *El Diario de Hoy* on February 22.

In his second deposition Miranda repeats his admission of membership in the ERP and participation in acts of sabotage, but corroborates the account given by his family of his activities on the days surrounding the murder, thereby denying any role. He says he knew Anaya from his Bible study group which met at a National University extension building, but did not know if Anaya also belonged to "a subversive group."

At the Zacamil Battalion, where he was first taken, Miranda says he was held blindfolded, beaten, a rag stuffed in his mouth that he supposed contained lime -- "which produced a parched and bitter sensation in his palate."[353] Constantly interrogated about his activities and affiliations, he was transferred blindfolded to what he believes was the National Police, where he was examined by people who identified themselves as a doctor and nurse. The day after his capture, he was given the first of several injections "for tonsilitis" over a couple of days. "I felt no positive reaction to the injections," he told the judge, "and felt weaker each day."[354]

Miranda says he led his captors to several locations where weapons were hidden. When "asked about several assassinations, among them that of Mr. Herbert Anaya Sanabria, and faced with the persistence of [the interrogators], he accepted his participation and began to say different invented facts about the act...."

The Official Story

In his first confession Miranda provided the pseudonyms of his two co-conspirators, the driver and the gunman, both members of his ERP cell, he said. On March 1, 1988 then Minister

---

[353]Declaracion Indagatoria, February 20, 1988, Centro Penal, "La Esperanza," Aytuxtepeque, #789.

[354]Declaracion Indagatoria, February 20, 1988, #791A.

of the Economy, Jose Ricardo Perdomo, in his capacity as acting president of the Commission on Investigations,[355] announced that Miranda Arevalo had identified the two men from police photos. Both had since been killed in combat.[356]

U.S. and Salvadoran officials interviewed by the Lawyers Committee expressed confidence that "good police work" had identified "the right man." A U.S. Embassy official said Miranda's retraction was not signifcant since "he didn't change all his testimony, just a tiny part of it."[357] This sentiment was echoed by Salvadoran officials in the justice system.[358]

Asked why the FMLN would have waited over eight months to kill Anaya if they believed him to have been passing information to the military since his release from prison in February 1987, a U.S. official said "it was politically brilliant to wait that long. They couldn't get another martyr any other way. Every day they were trying to entice the riot police."

Justice Minister Samayoa said the left's advance planning for demonstrations after the murder provided further proof of ERP culpability. "The left had plans to react, they had pamphlets printed up and demonstration times set. They had press communiques ready

---

[355]According to Article 2 of the law creating the body, the Commission is made up of three members: the Minister of Justice, Julio Alfredo Samayoa; the Vice-Minister of the Interior, Carmen Amelia Barohona de Morales; and a functionary of the Executive Branch designated by the President, in this case, former Economy Minister Jose Ricardo Perdomo. *Ley de Creacion de la Comision de Investigacion de Hechos Delictivos*, p.3.

[356]*El Mundo*, March 2, 1988; *La Prensa Grafica*, March 2, 1988.

[357]Lawyers Committee interview at the U.S. Embassy, May 23, 1988.

[358]Judge Luis Edgar Morales told members of a mission from Federation Internationale des Droits de L'Homme that he gave no credence to Miranda's retraction. Further, when the French group told the judge of the existence of witnesses who had not been interviewed, he said he had "no interest in these witnesses...in a case he considered closed." See "Rapport Mission a El Salvador, Dossier Anaya Sanabria," p.28.

to send around the world." [359] Officials said the FMLN -- through Miranda's family and his attorneys -- had pressured him into changing his story.

Defense attorneys Luis Dagoberto Campos and Leonardo Ramirez Murcia were first permitted to see their client on January 20, 1988. They told the Lawyers Committee in January 1989 that during the previous year they had only been allowed a couple of private interviews with Miranda; other meetings were attended by prison guards.[360]

On September 20 and 22, 1988, the Lawyers Committee and Americas Watch wrote to Justice Minister Samayoa requesting permission to visit Jorge Alberto Miranda Arevalo at Mariona prison. Neither the letters nor repeated follow-up telephone inquiries were answered.[361]

In a January 1989 summary of the case, Amnesty International offered the following conclusions:[362]

Because Jorge Miranda has since withdrawn his original confession, because of the internal contradictions within it, the discrepancies between it, other statements made by the prisoner and the physical evidence available on the case, and noting other information made available by relatives and witnesses, Amnesty International believes there is reason to doubt whether Jorge Miranda's extrajudicial

---

[359]Lawyers Committee interview with Justice Minister Julio Alfredo Samayoa, Ministry of Justice, September 1988.

[360]See "Mission a El Salvador," p.26. The judge denies that this is the case.

[361]Three U.S. reporters interviewed Miranda after his first confession. To the knowledge of the Lawyers Committee, only the French rights monitoring group, Federation Internationale des Droits de l'Homme, has been permitted to visit Miranda in prison. Since then he has only been visited by his family and attorneys, usually with a prison guard present.

[362]"El Salvador: Continued Detention Without Trial of Jorge Miranda Arevalo," Amnesty International, January 1989. (AMR 29/04/89).

statement is sufficient evidence on which to conclude that Jorge Miranda was indeed involved in the murder of Herbert Anaya. And, other than his supposed confession, Amnesty International understands that the government's case ....is virtually unsubstantiated.

Furthermore, the history of abuses directed against Herbert Anaya and his family, including his own arrest and alleged torture in May 1986, subsequent threats and intimidation directed at him by official security force personnel following his release, and the short-term detention of his 65-year-old father in March 1987, coupled with repeated accounts of security force harassment of other human rights monitors, constitute in Amnesty International's view cause for concern that official forces may have been responsible for his killing.

The organization is also concerned that Jorge Miranda continues to be held on the basis of a confession he has since withdrawn, and that there appears to have been no progress in the legal proceedings against him despite the fact that he has now spent well over a year in untried detention.

UNTS leader Humberto Centeno, right, assessing damage to the offices of the National Unity of Salvadoran Workers after a bomb exploded in April 1988. (photo: Corinne Dufka)

C. OTHER TARGETED SECTORS

According to Father Segundo Montes, director of the Jesuit University's Human Rights Institute, 213 Salvadorans were killed during 1988, with agricultural workers leading the list, followed by cooperativists and students.[363] The country's rural movement is among those sectors singled out for attack, as landlords and the military attempt to roll back the agrarian reform, impede organizing efforts by peasant unions and the FMLN, and block *campesino* access to technical support services.

According to Tutela Legal, Roberto Rodriquez Campos, a 56-year-old agrarian technician, was detained on June 1, 1988 by two heavily armed men in civilian clothing who were hooded.[364] Rodriquez and his driver were on a farm known as Santa Elena in Santa Tecla when they were stopped and ordered from the car. The driver was allowed to depart on foot; Rodriquez was shot near the vehicle. Summoned to the National Guard to give their statement, the victim's family was told by a Guard officer that he had interviewed Rodriquez a few days earlier and was aware he was collaborating with the FMLN. Rodriquez had been detained twice before, once by soldiers of the Atlacatl Battalion.

The labor movement is another sector facing serious harassment, at times violent.[365] On March 4, 1989, the bodies of two trade unionists were exhumed from a common, unmarked grave in Soyapango cemetery.[366] Miguel Angel Lazo Quintanilla, 35, a high school teacher of business administration and accounting, was a member of several teachers' unions. The National Association of Teachers of El Salvador (ANDES 21 de Junio) blamed his killing on

---

[363] El Salvador's Chanel 6 TV, January 12, 1989, as reported in "El Salvador Chronology," Vol. IV, No. 1, January 1989 (El Rescate Human Rights Department), pp.14-15.

[364] Tutela Legal Weekly Report, June 3-9, 1988, p.17.

[365] See *Labor Rights in El Salvador* (Americas Watch, March 1988).

[366] Summary of the cases prepared for the Lawyers Committee, March 16, 1989. A Lawyers Committee representative was present at the exhumation.

the Air Force.[367] The second victim, Carlos Rodriquez Dominguez, a 22-year-old mechanic, was a member of the Salvadoran Unitarian Unionists' Federation (FUSS). Tutela Legal said death squads were responsible for both killings.[368]

One federation particulary hard-hit is the militant National Unity of Salvadoran Workers (UNTS). Following is an account of the illegal detention and beating of UNTS leader Humberto Centeno, who was "sentenced to death" by the Maximiliano Hernandez Martinez Anti-Communist Brigade in late February 1989. On February 8, the UNTS headquarters were shot at by men in a vehicle. On February 15, a high-powered bomb exploded at 3:50 a.m. in the union's offices; an anti-communist urban commando took responsibility for the attack.

On July 12, 1988, Eliseo Cordova Aguilar, Vice-President of the STISSS union of social security workers, a UNTS-affiliate, became the seventh STISSS worker to disappear since 1981.[369] Cordova, his nephew, and a friend -- a lawyer who works in the Attorney General's office -- were abducted by armed hooded men, who later released the youth and the attorney. The lawyer's wife was told by the Treasury Police that her husband and the boy would be released unharmed. Eliseo Cordova remains disappeared.

---

[367]*La Prensa Grafica*, February 25, 1989; *El Mundo*, February 25, 1989.

[368]Tutela Legal Weekly Report, February 17-23, 1989.

[369]See "Report on the Situation in El Salvador," Department of State, December 1, 1988, p.13; the testimony of Cordova's nephew, Enemias Hernandez, who was abducted with him, was recorded by the Lawyers Committee in San Salvador on January 7, 1989.

Humberto Centeno
March 10, 1988

Attack by the Air Force

At approximately 11:00 a.m. on March 10, 1988 some 50 members of the Workers Solidarity Coordinating Committee (CST), a labor group affiliated with the National Unity of Salvadoran Workers (UNTS), the country's largest opposition federation, arrived at the Ministry of Labor for a meeting with Labor Minister Dr. Lazaro Tadeo Bernal Lizama.[370]

A scuffle broke out with ministry guards when workers attempted to enter the minister's office. According to the workers' testimony, a guard threw a chair through a window, resulting in minor injuries to Dr. Bernal Lizama. The minister -- meeting at the time with representatives of the Archdiocese, including Msgr. Modesto Lopez Portillo[371] -- immediately left the ministry through the window. Msgr. Lopez Portillo remained at the labor office, later serving as mediator with Auxiliary Bishop Msgr. Gregorio Rosa Chavez, who arrived on the scene in the late afternoon. Apprised of what the minister termed an "occupation" of his office, members of the Air Force and Treasury Police surrounded the building, trapping the workers inside. When they received news of the encirclement, other trade unionists began to gather outside the ministry, along the Panamerican Highway in Ilopango.

Among those unionists was 47-year-old Humberto Centeno, journalist and secretary general of the Salvadoran Telecommunications Workers Association (ASTTEL). Centeno told the Lawyers Committee that he arrived at the scene about 4:30 p.m., with colleagues and some 15 North American visitors. The group was prohibited from approaching the ministry by a police roadblock a few hundred yards down the Panamerican in the direction of San

---

[370]According to UNTS leader Humberto Centeno, CST representatives had made an appointment with the Labor Minister, who was nonetheless surprised and alarmed by the number of people who showed up, and refused to receive the group. (Lawyers Committee interview, May 20, 1988, at UNTS office, San Salvador.)

[371] Tutela Legal, as cited in "Letter to the Churches," April 1-15, 1988.

Salvador. Some 100 unionists stood talking in front of Cafe Listo, an instant coffee factory.[372]

Centeno recalls that about 6:30 p.m., an Air Force lieutenant addressed him by name, saying he had orders from Air Force chief Gen. Rafael Bustillo to disperse the gathering. "I told him that since there was no State of Emergency in effect and we weren't blocking traffic, we had every right to gather," recalls Centeno.[373]

The lieutenant left, but soon returned with three trucks carrying between 50 and 100 uniformed soldiers. According to Centeno, he was grabbed, beaten, handcuffed and packed off to nearby Ilopango Air Base in one of the trucks.

A canvas hood smelling of gasoline was placed over Centeno's head. Though he did not resist arrest, the beating continued and he was repeatedly hit in the head with a boot and a rifle butt. Stripped to his underwear, Centeno says he was told by members of the Air Force that they planned to kill all UNTS members because "Duarte can't stand you."

Centeno says that he soon lost consciousness, awakening en route to what he believes was the *Estado Mayor*, the High Command of the Armed Forces. By midnight he found himself in the headquarters of the Treasury Police where he was examined by a doctor. About an hour later he was transferred to Centro de Diagnostico, a private San Salvador hospital.

At 8:30 a.m. on the morning of March 11, Centeno was examined by Dr. Francisco Hernandez Martinez, a surgeon associated with the governmental Human Rights Commission of El

---

[372]Account based on interview with Lawyers Committee, May 20, 1988; Centeno's complaint to Fourth Penal Judge, San Salvador; and report of the governmental Human Rights Commission (CDH), March 12, 1988.

[373]Article 7 of the Constitution of the Republic of El Salvador of 1983 reads in part: "Salvadoran residents have the right to associate freely and to peacefully gather, unarmed, for any legal objective."

Salvador (CDH).[374]   Dr. Hernandez' report indicates that he found the patient badly bruised about the chest and abdomen, with multiple superficial lacerations on the limbs.   In his report to the Director General of the Treasury Police, Dr. Hernandez concluded that Centeno had been subjected to "multiple uncomplicated traumas," and recommended that he be kept under observation for the next 48 hours "to follow the development of the case."[375]

Alerted by a nurse that he was hospitalized at the Centro de Diagnostico, Centeno's wife, Milagro del Rosario Lopez de Centeno, confirmed her husband's whereabouts with the Treasury Police and visited him. He was released to his family and union colleagues the next day.[376]

---

[374]Despite the participation of a governmental Human Rights Commission (CDH) doctor, the CDH placed a statement in newspapers published Friday, March 11, 1988 condemning the physical attack on the Minister of Labor. The statement deplored the unionists' violent methods and said it had informed the United Nations Human Rights Commission in Geneva, the Inter-American Human Rights Commission, and other international organizations. No mention was made of the beating and arbitrary arrest of Centeno, which CDH head Benjamin Cestoni finally acknowledged later that day.

[375]Letter from Dr. Juan Antonio Portillo Hernandez to Senor Director General de la Policia de Hacienda, March 11, 1988. When Centeno's wife and daughter first visited him at Centro de Diagnostico the labor leader was receiving intravenous feeding and was attached to a catheter.

[376]Over 300 telegrams were sent by U.S. trade unionists protesting the beating, and New York unionists placed an advertisement in El Mundo. (Interview with Dave Dyson, Director, Union Label Department, Amalgamated Clothing and Textile Workers Union and of the National Labor Committee in Support of Democracy and Human Rights in El Salvador, October 24, 1988.)
Canadian diplomats, on instructions from their Department of External Affairs, registered a protest. (Telephone interview with an official in the Canadian Department of External Affairs, November 15, 1988.)
The costs of Centeno's three-day hospitalization were covered by the Treasury Police. Interviewed by the Lawyers Committee over two months after the assault, the labor leader said he still had frequent headaches and could not digest certain foods.

On May 27, Centeno filed a complaint with Fourth Penal Judge Ricardo Alberto Zamora Perez of San Salvador.[377]

Centeno's signed complaint describes his physical condition after the attack; the theft of 600 *colones* (ca. $130), a $30 Parker pen, and a gold plaque of sentimental value honoring him for 25 years of service to ANTEL, the telecommunications company; the use of force and loss of liberty. Cited to appear as witnesses are Air Force Chief Gen. Rafael Bustillo; the head of the High Command of the Armed Forces at the time, Gen. Adolfo Onecifero Blandon; and several eyewitnesses to the capture and subsequent events.

Interviewed on January 12, 1989, Judge Ricardo A. Zamora of San Salvador's Fourth Penal Court, where the case is being heard, said only Gen. Bustillo had been asked to testify and according to Article 205 of the Criminal Procedure Code he could give a written statement, though he had not yet done so. Dr. Zamora suggested the case would not progress since Centeno was not able to identify his attackers.[378]

Centeno's case was also brought before the Inter-American Commission of Human Rights of the Organization of American

---

[377]The Criminal Procedure Code specifies two ways in which an investigation into an alleged crime can be launched in El Salvador: 1. By Denunciation or Accusation -- A private citizen can file a complaint stating the facts and asking for an official investigation of a crime. If the judge finds sufficient evidence that a crime has been committed, he or she opens the case (Article 146). 2. Ex Officio -- If a First Instance Judge or a Justice of the Peace has personal knowledge of an alleged crime, he/she is required to launch an investigation(Article 147). As Auxiliary Organs of the Court, the Security Forces are also authorized to launch an investigation, according to Articles 137 and 138 of the Criminal Procedure Code.
The attack on Centeno was well covered in Salvadoran media and therefore well known, which in its own right should have triggered an official investigation. No judicial authority took action, however, until the victim filed a complaint over two months after the attack.

[378]Lawyers Committee interview with Judge Ricardo A. Zamora, Fourth Penal Court, San Salvador, January 12, 1989.

States, but as of early February 1989, the OAS had not responded.[379 & 380]

[379]Lawyers Committee interview with Centeno, September 29, 1988 and follow-up, February 1989.

[380]According to court documents reviewed by the Human Rights Institute of the Central American University Jose Simeon Canas (IDHUCA), Labor Minister Lazaro Tadeo Bernal Lizama filed a criminal complaint with the Justice of the Peace in Ilopango at 3:30 p.m. on March 10, that is, *while* the unionists were still inside the ministry. Provisional detention orders were issued on March 12 for four participants in the action for the "crimes of very serious injuries against the Minister" (Art.172(5), of Penal Code); "aggravated damages of the installation" (Art. 254(3); and "acts of terrorism" (Art. 400(4)). On March 14, 1988, the case was remitted to the Fourth Penal Court, San Salvador.

At 6:30 p.m., after the unionists had been removed to buses outside the ministry, Msgr. Gregorio Rosa Chavez, San Salvador's Auxiliary Bishop, inspected the ministry accompanied by the Justice of the Peace of Ilopango, his secretary, and a Treasury Police official. According to the court documents reviewed by IDHUCA on May 18, 1988, the inspection turned up no signs of violence or ransacking. The unionists had written graffiti on the walls of the Minister's office and a second floor office. Election leaflets and empty fried chicken cartons were left behind; a part was removed from a radio rendering it nonfunctional; and on the second floor telephone lines had been disconnected.

One year later, on March 16, 1989, one of the four unionists, Juan Jose Huezo, was detained by the National Police at 9:30 a.m. near the office of FENASTRES (the National Federation of Salvadoran Workers), on whose board he served. He was charged with acts of terrorism; arms trafficking; armed assault on the Minister of Labor; sabotage of the national economy; and association with subversives. On arrival at Mariona prison on March 18, a medical examination revealed blows to the chest, head, and legs.

158

Manfredo Zuniga Lazo
and Maria Ana Saenz de Zuniga
April 16, 1988

The Attempted Murders

Manfredo Zuniga Lazo, 31, and his wife, Maria Ana Saenz de Zuniga, 32, were sprayed with gunfire as they drove up to their home in Santa Ana at 8:30 p.m. on April 16, 1988, according to interviews conducted with the couple by the Lawyers Committee in May 1988. Zuniga, an agronomist, and Saenz, an employee of the Ministry of Agriculture and Livestock (MAG), both worked at Ahuachapan's La Labor Agrarian Reform Co-operative created in 1980.

The co-op's yellow Nissan in which the couple was riding was surrounded by some 15-20 men in civilian clothing as one gunman approached the driver's side, hitting Saenz in the left eye. As Saenz fell through the open door to the sidewalk, her husband -- attempting to escape through the same door -- was felled by several bullets to his side and chest, fired from at least three different weapons, according to attending physicians.[381]

Neighbors, alerted by the victims' screams, immediately came to their aid, quickly enough to see the attackers flee in a waiting white vehicle. Zuniga and Lazo told the Lawyers Committee they saw some of the men get out of a white 1985 Datsun as they parked. Thanks to the neighbors' rapid response, the couple was immediately taken to the Santa Ana hospital for treatment. During their 15-day hospitalization, the two were protected by friends in the military. Interviewed almost one month after the attack by U.S. human rights workers, the couple could still not sit up in bed. The bullets had not yet been removed from Saenz' head and Zuniga still had at least one projectile lodged near his spine and another in his right shoulder.

On April 21, a few days after the attempted murders, unknown gunmen attacked the same car in which the couple had been riding when they were shot. The windshield and right window were destroyed, but none of the three co-op leaders who were in the car was injured. The couple and their two children, withdrawn

---

[381]The couple was interviewed by the Lawyers Committee while in hiding at the co-op on May 14, 1988.

from school on the advice of teachers, remained in hiding at the co-op until transport could be arranged out of the country. In late June, the family was granted asylum in Australia.

The Possible Motive

According to FECORASAL, a federation of agrarian reform cooperatives,[382] La Labor is the only agrarian reform co-op on which the former owners still reside. One complex of buildings on the 6,800 acre farm includes the *hacienda* house, occupied by the former owners, their office, and the co-op office.

La Labor was formed in 1980 by 829 cooperativists, all of whom were *colonos* or tenants on the heretofore privately owned *hacienda*. Until 1987, the cooperative board was dominated by the former overseers, who blocked free elections. Government extension agents employed by MAG were threatened while working at La Labor in 1980 and 1981. When their names turned up on a list of subversives, they left the country.[383]

The Salaverria Lagos family, protected by their own bodyguards, were granted approximately 180 acres by the Supreme Court in 1986, citing a provision in the reform legislation providing partial relief for expropriated landowners. Co-op members say they have access to under half of the original 6,800 acres on the Salaverria's *hacienda*. The family uses the rest. The peasants also say that the former owners were awarded the farm's coffee processing plant in 1985, in contravention of the law.

MAG experts continued to assist the *cooperativistas*; a restructuring of the co-op board eventually led to free elections and ouster of the leadership. The day after the new board was installed, a 42-year-old co-op member was murdered by unidentified men, the *cooperativistas* told a Lawyers Committee

---

[382]FECORASAL is an independent federation operating in the western part of El Salvador. FECORASAL spokespeople say the organization is not affiliated with either of the large labor federations, the opposition UNTS or the Christian Democratic UNOC, though the federation has participated in Christian Democratic activities along with UNOC.

[383]This account is based on interviews conducted with the family and unionists by a Lawyers Committee representative.

representative. The board president, followed and threatened with death, resigned and fled to the United States.

In January 1988, Manfredo Zuniga Lazo was hired as farm manager and his wife continued to work on a volunteer basis. A few weeks before the murder attempt, Maria Ana Saenz de Zuniga helped the *campesinos* rent well-cleaning equipment from the government. The couple said a Salaverria put a 45 to the head of a 42-year-old co-op man working on the well, threatening to kill him for taking the water. Saenz had on several occasions sought help from friends in government and the military.

No Investigation

At the hospital shortly after the attack, Saenz remembers a National Police detective trying to question her. "Don't die, lady!" she recalls him saying, "Give us clues!" She was only able to moan that they had no enemies.

Since that interview no further investigation has been conducted, to the knowledge of the couple and FECORASAL. Alerted by a paid advertisement placed by the cooperative federation in a San Salvador daily, U.S. human rights workers visited the couple in hiding.

Based on interviews with officials at the Ministry of Justice and the Attorney General's office, the Lawyers Committee has concluded that no investigation was conducted. Neither the couple nor judicial authorities initiated court proceedings.

D. CONDITIONS IN DETENTION

In January 1987, El Salvador's six-year-old State of Emergency lapsed on its own terms. As a result, administrative detention was restricted to the first 72 hours after arrest, reduced significantly from the 15 days allowed under emergency procedures. Unfortunately this constitutional safeguard is not being respected in practice. The Lawyers Committee continues to receive well documented reports that political suspects are being arrested and detained for periods well in excess of 72 hours.[384] The Lawyers Committee is also concerned that in a number of cases, prisoners continue to be subjected to cruel and inhuman treatment by security force officers, including physical torture.

In his report to the United Nations, Special Representative Jose Antonio Pastor Ridruejo concluded:

As in previous years, the Special Representative has encountered cases of intense psychological pressure amounting to cruel, inhuman or degrading treatment during police interrogation of political detainees.[385]

Though Professor Pastor Ridruejo reports that he did not interview enough detainees "to establish precisely what percentage were subjected to ill-treatment and psychological pressure," he concluded that "there is no generalized practice of psychological

---

[384]The State Department's April 1988 "Report on the Situation in El Salvador" stated that the Salvadoran Armed Forces "lobbied hard with both the President and the Assembly in favor of the state of seige but was rebuffed. Although disappointed and in disagreement with this decision of the civilian government, the [Armed Forces] accepted it.

"More importantly, in practice [the military] demonstrated its acceptance. Security force and military units ceased exercising the emergency powers granted them under Decree 50 as soon as it expired. Instead, they began to follow the due process procedures called for by the 1983 constitution," p.17. The State Department's assertion does not coincide with fact-finding conducted by the Lawyers Committee and other human rights monitors.

[385]"Informe Definitivo," paragraph 101, p.23.

162

maltreatment."[386] Instead he found that some detainees are singled out for abusive treatment based on a number of factors, including the potential value of their information, who their captors are, and the military situation at that moment. Among the forms of mistreatment that he reported were "being kept blindfolded for long periods of time, deprived of food for many hours, subjected to various forms of beatings and threats, and prevented from sleeping or even lying or sitting down, for long periods."

In its annual human rights report to the U.S. Congress, published in February 1989, the U.S. Department of State concluded:

> Reports of abuse by arresting forces continue, with most involving abuses that leave no marks and thus are extremely difficult to prove or disprove. Such abuses include deprivation of food and sleep, threats against the detainee or his family, prolonged interrogation while blindfolded, being forced to stand for long periods of time, forced exercise, and blows to the ears. Some prisoners claim to have been forced to sign confessions without being permitted to read them. Some instances of severe beatings, rape, choking, injection with unidentified drugs, and electric shock were reported.[387]

Based on our own monitoring of conditions in El Salvador, we have identified a pattern of psychological as well as physical abuse of detainees. One recent case of physical abuse was reported to the Lawyers Committee in early 1989. It involves four *campesinos* who were picked up by uniformed members of the Salvadoran Army in early December 1988. All four men, Rosabel Sibrian Nunez, 31; Amadeo Lopez, 25; Consuelo Ayala, 18; and Manuel Cartagena, 37, were taken to the Fourth Infantry Brigade Headquarters at El Paraiso in Chalatenango province. All four are residents of communities in northern Chalatenango that have recently been repopulated by displaced persons. The men were removed from vehicles belonging to the Archdiocese of San Salvador and the UN High Commissioner for Refugees.

---

[386]*Ibid.*, paragraph 68, p.16.

[387]"Country Reports on Human Rights for 1988," Submitted to the Committee on Foreign Relations, U.S. Senate, and Committee on Foreign Affairs, U.S. House of Representatives, by the Department of State, February 1989, p.557.

According to their statements, the four men were tied up, forced to take off their clothes, and were interrogated at knifepoint by the soldiers. As they were being interrogated, they were repeatedly beaten and kicked, and at one stage they were hung from the ceiling with their hands tied tightly behind their backs. The interrogation and beatings occurred over a three-day period. One detainee testified that he was visited during that period by two English-speaking men. On December 4, they were transported in a brown pick-up truck without license plates to the National Guard headquarters in San Salvador, accompanied by three armed men in civilian clothing. Two of the detainees were released on December 5; the remaining two were released on December 8.[388]

In other cases, including three which are summarized below, detainees or prisoners have died in custody. Two of the detainees in these case studies died following severe physical abuse. To our knowledge there have been no serious investigations or prosecutions undertaken in any of these cases.

---

[388]Summary of the case prepared for the Lawyers Committee, February 13, 1989.

Jose Angel Alas Gomez
January 12, 1988

Detention and Death

Jose Angel Alas Gomez, 27, was found dead on January 12, 1988, slumped in the back seat of a police vehicle parked at the San Salvador headquarters of the Treasury Police. The medical examiner's report cites "cardiac arrest" as the cause of death. It contains little other information or analysis of the cause of death. Dr. Carlos Humberto Orellana Gomez said Alas' heart had stopped after he suffered several "traumas": "superficial ecchymosis of both cheekbones and the chin; superficial ecchymosis on the back and shoulders; superficial laceration on the left knee and the small of the back."[389]

Copies of photos of Alas' body provided to the Lawyers Committee by the nongovernmental Human Rights Commission indicate blows to the head, shoulders and testicles, and burns on his back and shoulders. These photographs also appeared on Salvadoran television.

Alas, who worked as a mechanic, was detained on January 11, 1988 when the car in which he was riding was stopped by the Treasury Police on the highway between Sonsonate and Armenia; two other men escaped from the car, which none of them owned.

His 19-year-old widow, Sara Ordonez, told the Lawyers Committee on September 27, 1988 that the victim had first been detained on December 27, 1987 by soldiers of the Atlacatl Battalion, who accused him of theft and subversive activity. She says that her husband was beaten and tortured with electric shock on his feet, hands and tongue, and finally released on December 31.[390]

---

[389]"Reconocimiento" filed January 12, 1988 by Dr. Carlos Humberto Orellana Gomez with Second Justice of the Peace, San Salvador; ecchymosis indicates the passage of blood from ruptured blood vessels into subcutaneous tissue, marked by a purple discoloration of the skin.

[390]Lawyers Committee interview with Sara Ordonez and Yanira Alas Gomez, sister of Jose Angel Alas Gomez, Canton Lourdes, La Libertad, September 27, 1988.

165

Alarmed when Alas Gomez did not return to their home in the village of Lourdes, La Libertad province on January 11, the family first learned what had happened when his death was reported on the radio.

The victim's sister, Yanira Alas Gomez, 19, told the Lawyers Committee that she was also detained on November 27, 1987 by uniformed members of the Atlacatl Battalion. She recalls that the soldiers had knocked on the door about 1:00 a.m., asking for her brothers. When she told them they were not at home, the men said they would take her instead.[391]

She says she was taken in a beige Ford pick-up to the battalion headquarters and finally released on December 19 from the Colon prison. During her capture she was doused in ice water, sprayed with gasoline and kept blindfolded for most of eight days. Her captors repeatedly threatened to take her to *El Playon*, notorious death squad dumping ground, and kill her. Yanira Alas Gomez says members of the governmental Human Rights Commission photographed her in Colon prison, where she says she was not mistreated. On release, soldiers warned Alas Gomez against publicizing her experience.

According to accounts in the local press, Jose Angel Alas Gomez was detained by the Treasury Police because he was a suspect in an extortion ring. The injuries leading to his death occurred when the suspect tried to flee the custody of the police, Salvadoran newspapers reported. [392]

---

[391]Lawyers Committee interview with Yanira Alas Gomez, September 27, 1988, Canton Lourdes.

[392]*El Latino*, undated, and *El Diario de Hoy*, January 14, 1988.

Gerardo Hernandez Torres
December 16, 1988

Detention, Torture and Death

According to the former warden of La Esperanza or Mariona Prison, Francisco Olmedo, an inspection of the political section by members of the National Police was arranged at the request of Minister of Justice Julio Alfredo Samayoa, who said he wished to renovate the quarters. The inspection was carried out in late November 1987 with the cooperation of COPPES, the Committee of Political Prisoners of El Salvador. Several days later the Minister inspected the section himself, accompanied by journalists.

On December 11 and 12, 1987 Gerardo Hernandez Torres, 27, Vladimir Guzman Rosales and Jose Guadalupe Dominguez, both 17, were detained by the Atlacatl Battalion on or near the Oakland coffee plantation in San Ramon in the jurisdiction of Mejicanos. Hernandez Torres worked in the bakery of his mother, who testified that soldiers forceably removed her son from their home at 2:00 a.m. on Saturday, December 12, 1987. The men -- who threatened to explode a bomb if Feliciana Torres de Hernandez, 63, did not open the door -- ransacked the house "in search of her son's weapons." They also stole $194 she had hidden under a cotton blanket to be used for baking supplies.[393]

One soldier also raped Hernandez Torres' 24-year-old sister, Maria Olivia Hernandez Torres, who filed a complaint with the Justice of the Peace in Ayutuxtepeque on December 16, 1987.[394]

The three were transferred to First Brigade Headquarters on the morning of December 12 and turned over that evening to the National Police, where they were interrogated and extrajudicial confessions recorded. On December 15, they were taken to the First Penal Court in San Salvador to give judicial declarations before Judge Luis Edgar Morales Joya.

---

[393]Declaracion de Ofendido, Juzgado de Paz, Ayutuxtepeque, 11:00 a.m., December 17, 1987.

[394]Tutela Legal #01789 and Declaracion de Ofendido, Juzgado de Paz, 1:40 p.m., December 17, 1987.

167

Feliciana Torres de Hernandez told the Human Rights Office of the Archdiocese of San Salvador that she encountered her son by chance when she went to the courts to enlist legal aid for his case. During a brief conversation, her son, whose eyes were red, said he had been tortured extensively: electric shock to the tongue which had caused him to faint; hot rods down his throat; a rubber hood or *capucha* doused in chalk had been placed over his head to cause suffocation. Mrs. Hernandez also gave this account on Salvadoran television.

The account of Hernandez Torres' torture was corroborated by the two men detained with him, both of whom overheard his cries and protests.[395] Vladmir Guzman Rosales told the Human Rights Office of the Central American University that he heard soldiers throw Hernandez Torres down some steps and overheard him say it would be better if they killed him immediately rather than apply electric shocks. Guzman Rosales says he was also subjected to electric shock.

A common prisoner assigned to receive new inmates testified that Hernandez Torres was incoherent and walked with difficulty as though drunk when he arrived at Mariona Prison on December 15. His hands were badly swollen with deep cuts on his thumbs from wires. Blood was visible in his eyes, which were nearly swollen shut. Hernandez Torres said he had been hung by his hands and that he had asked to be taken to a hospital, but his request was denied.

According to a letter dated April 25, 1988 from J. Edward Fox, Assistant Secretary of State for Legislative Affairs, to Sen. Mark Hatfield, Chairman of the Arms Control and Foreign Policy Caucus of the U.S. Senate, the three men were visited on December 14 by a "delegate from the governmental Human Rights Commission (CDH)...[who] found them to be in good condition, although they alleged that First Brigade troops had 'roughed them up.'"

The three prisoners were told that the political section was empty and were therefore assigned to the common section. Discovering that 17 prisoners were still held in the political section, the three joined them. During that night Hernandez Torres acted

---

[395]This account is based on interviews conducted by the Human Rights Institute of the Central American University, Jose Simeon Canas (IDHUCA) on December 17, 1987 and the Institute's review of court files on the case.

irrationally, yelling for his family, saying the walls were coming down around him and that he saw blood. At one point he picked up a stick and threatened to hit the other prisoners. Around dawn he calmed down and went to sleep. By 6:45 that morning he was dead.

The medical examination conducted by Dr. Rodolfo Huezo Melara at the request of the Seventh Justice of the Peace of San Salvador found trauma [blood] in the left eye; bruises on his left side; lesions on the bottoms of the feet; lacerations on both thumbs; internal bleeding in the left ventricle of the heart; and an enlarged liver. Dr. Huezo Melara concluded his report with the following statement: "I am of the opinion that death was caused by multiple traumas which provoked cardiac failure, respiratory failure."[396]

Salvadoran government officials told the Lawyers Committee that they believed Hernandez Torres was beaten to death by fellow inmates,[397] an assertion echoed by U.S. Embassy officials. Assistant Secretary Fox's letter to Senator Hatfield says that the autopsy of Hernandez revealed "external injuries which were not evident at the time Hernandez appeared before the magistrate. The origin of the injuries remains unknown."

The State Department letter continued: "Given the severity of Hernandez' injury, it is highly improbable that he would not have shown intense pain during his audience with the magistrate, had he been injured while in police custody. An investigation by the Salvadoran Attorney General's office into the cause of Hernandez' death is underway."

Auxiliary Bishop Gregorio Rosa Chavez denounced Hernandez Torres' death in the weekly homily on December 20, 1987. The Bishop said, "The autopsy shows clearly that he died as

---

[396]Court documents reviewed by IDHUCA, December 1987.

[397]In an article appearing in *La Prensa Grafica* on December 23, 1987, Justice Minister Samayoa suggested that other political prisoners were responsible for Hernandez' death. "I'm not accusing anyone, it's only a conjecture," he said. As cited in El Rescate Chronology, Volume II, No.12, December 1987.

a result of the tortures. Does this mean we are returning to the dark methods of the past?"[398]

---

[398]*El Mundo*, December 21, 1987, as cited in El Rescate Chronology, Volume II, No.12, December 1987.

Manuel de Jesus Araujo Sanchez
December 19, 1987

Manuel de Jesus Araujo Sanchez died during an assault on Mariona Prison by a U.S.-trained SWAT team. The circumstances surrounding his death remain unclear. Dr. Samayoa told the Lawyers Committee that because the political prisoners had destroyed the facilities and denied access to the renovation team, he issued orders to disperse the remaining 17 detainees throughout the country. "They were a very aggressive group, especially those involved in the Zona Rosa," he said in explaining why he decided to carry out a "surprise operation."[399] Warden Francisco Olmedo testified that Samayoa was furious that the men had joined the political section and told Olmedo by phone that he intended to dissolve the unit.[400]

Around 2:00 a.m. on December 19, 1987 an elite assault team blew open the door of the political section of the prison.[401]

---

[399]Lawyers Committee interview, July 15, 1988, San Salvador. Tutela Legal, "Informe especial sobre los hechos ocurridos en el centro penitenciario La Esperanza, ubicado en canton San Luis Mariona, Ayutuxtepeque, San Salvador, El Dia 19 de Diciembre de 1987."

[400]Assistant Secretary Fox offers yet another explanation of the assault on Mariona: "As a result of the Hernandez death in the COPPES cellblock, President Duarte ordered Justice Minister Samayoa to remove the few remaining COPPES prisoners from Mariona Prison, disperse them throughout other penal facilities around the country, and reassert the prison authorities' control of the COPPES cellblock." Letter to Senator Hatfield, April 25, 1988.

[401]According to Assistant Secretary Fox, the assault was conducted by a U.S.-trained SWAT team, the Special Antiterrorist Commando Squad (CEAT). "The CEAT is an elite military unit whose members are drawn from armed forces and security forces ranks. It has no law enforcement or police functions. As such, it receives training and equipment through the regular military assistance program, and some personnel have received training through the Anti-Terrorism Assistance Program." Letter from J. Edward Fox, Assistant Secretary of State for Legislative Affairs, to Sen. Mark O. Hatfield, Chairman, Arms Control and Foreign Policy Caucus, United States Senate, April 25, 1988.

171

Frightened by the explosion, the prisoners jumped out of bed and ran into the courtyard, where they were surrounded by troops in olive green or black uniforms, some masked, armed with firearms and clubs. The detainees -- clothed in their underwear -- were tied up and placed in two lines facing one another; some were repeatedly kicked.

A roll-call revealed that one prisoner was missing. Manuel de Jesus Araujo was first spotted some hours laters on a terrace above the section by guards, who went up after him. The prisoners seated below then heard a few shots, and later learned that Araujo was dead. The remaining detainees were permitted to dress and gather belongings from their rooms. They testified that their cells had been searched and ransacked, and things were missing.

The Explanation

Officials say Araujo Sanchez threw himself head first off the terrace, committing suicide. The Justice of the Peace of Ayutuxtepeque identified the body at 7:40 a.m. on December 19, 1987. His report describes multiple scrapes and a head wound, and offers the opinion that the cause of death was trauma to the head as a result of the fall. An autopsy was not conducted.[402]

On January 8, nearly three weeks after the death, the same Justice of the Peace took statements from two prison guards who said they saw the jump. One said Araujo Sanchez came running down the balcony with his hands in the air and then dove off, "like someone who dives into the water."[403]

Calling him a "fanatic," Justice Minister Samayoa said Araujo Sanchez refused to come down when ordered and said they would only take him dead. "Politically it was important to be able to say he had been assassinated," Samayoa told the Lawyers Committee in a July 1988 interview. "The political section functioned for eight years and we've never had such disorder [una desorden asi]. They had their own law. It can be verified."

---

[402]Reconocimiento, Justice of the Peace of Ayutuxtepeque, December 19, 1987.

[403]Declaracion de Testigo, Jose Luis Zaldana Diaz, January 8, 1988 to Justice of Peace, Ayutuxtepeque and the testimony of Felipe Hernandez Mejia to the same justice.

Samayoa also acknowledged the apparent difficulty of establishing the facts in cases such as this: "In this context of violence there are two truths -- the truth of the government and the truth of the enemies of the government. Many times people do not believe the authorities."

The Commission on Investigations has not looked into the death of Manuel de Jesus Araujo.[404]

---

[404]A report issued by the press office of the Armed Forces (COPREFA) said "The event took place when military authorities came to the prison to assist the Ministry of Justice in removing 17 prisoners who had taken over a sector. They had caused considerable material damages and it was necessary to make repairs. When the authorities entered they found weapons and propaganda. Araujo perished when he committed suicide throwing himself off the roof of the prison.The sixteen remaining prisoners have been sent to other prisons of the country to avoid more problems." *El Mundo*, December 21, 1987, as cited in El Rescate Chronology, Volume II, No. 12, December 1987.

The Aftermath of the Three Deaths in Detention

In its annual human rights country report, the State Department said the two December 1987 deaths at Mariona occurred "under mysterious circumstances" and that "both incidents are being investigated by the authorities."[405]

Assistant Secretary Fox's letter to Senator Hatfield concluded: "In summary, we do not believe the facts as currently known about either of these incidents give rise to any definitive presumptions of torture of prisoners by Salvadoran authorities. Should the report on Hernandez's [sic] death being prepared by the office of the Attorney General suggest wrongdoing by any unit or members of the Salvadoran security forces, we will take that information into account in selecting further participants for training programs for El Salvador. We do not feel it appropriate to inquire of the Government of El Salvador the names of arresting officers or their superiors in the absence of credible evidence of wrongdoing and, in the case of the Hernandez death, while competent Salvadoran officials are still conducting an investigation."

Lic. Arturo Lazo of the Attorney General's office told the Lawyers Committee on July 11, 1988 that his human rights unit had looked into the death of Hernandez Torres, but "nothing came of it." In late January 1989, a U.S. Embassy official told the Lawyers Committee that to his knowledge the Salvadoran government had never issued a report on the death of Gerardo Hernandez Torres.

Of the Araujo Sanchez death, Justice Minister Samayoa said on July 15, 1988 that his Special Investigative Unit had never conducted an investigation, indicating that he believed Araujo Sanchez had committed suicide.

In its 1988 report on human rights in El Salvador, the State Department listed the death of Jose Angel Alas Gomez in the section on torture and other cruel treatment: "The police blamed the

---

[405]*Country Report on Human Rights Practices for 1987*, El Salvador, Section C. on Torture and Other Cruel, Inhuman, or Degrading Treatment or Punishment (Department of State, February 1988) p. 478.

death on a heart attack brought on by a fall while trying to escape, but marks on the body cast doubt on this story."[406]

[406]*Country Reports on Human Rights Practices for 1988,* (Department of State, February 1989) p.557.

Student demonstrators detained at National Police headquarters, San Salvador, September 13, 1988. (photo: Corinne Dufka)

CHAPTER IV: POLICE TRAINING
Aid and Training for El Salvador's Security Forces

In 1974, Congress passed legislation which prohibited the U.S. government from training foreign police forces. Under AID's Office of Public Safety, over 500,000 police in 41 countries had been trained and equipped by the United States between 1962 and 1974.[407] AID's 12-year program in El Salvador trained some 300 high-ranking officers in the United States. According to a 1986 study by the congressional Arms Control and Foreign Policy Caucus, "Roughly half of AID's $2 million program provided equipment such as mobile radio units, vehicles, weapons, ammunition, riot helmets and tear gas grenades."[408]

AID is known to have been pleased with the program in El Salvador, citing it as a regional "model" in 1972.[409] Yet members of El Salvador's three Security Forces, which are part of the Armed Forces, were responsible for much of the worst death squad activities of the early 1980's, when there were more than 800 political killings each month. As the State Department acknowledged in April 1988, the Armed Forces were closely involved in death squad killings during this period:

> It is generally acknowledged that death squads of the right -- often comprised of active duty military or security force personnel operating with the complicity of some senior officers of the armed forces -- were responsible for thousands of murders.[410]

Among the U.S. trainees linked to these paramilitary groups are Maj. Roberto D'Aubuisson, founder of the right-wing ARENA party, who is believed to have ordered the 1980 murder of

---

[407]"Police Aid to Central America: Yesterday's Lessons, Today's Choices," Arms Control and Foreign Policy Caucus, August 13, 1986, p.4.

[408]*Ibid*, p.6.

[409]From testimony of AID's Public Safety Director before the House Committee on Appropriations, 1972, as cited in "Police Aid to Central America," p.6.

[410]"Report on the Situation in El Salvador," Pursuant to Section 561 of Public Law 100-202, April 1, 1988, p.22.

Archbishop Romero; Gen. Jose Alberto Medrano, founder of the rural paramilitary group, ORDEN, reportedly dismantled in the early 1980's; and Lt. Jose Antonio Castillo, head of an investigative unit at the National Guard.[411]

Congress dismantled the Public Safety program in 1974 in response to evidence that U.S. trainees in countries such as Iran, Vietnam, Brazil and El Salvador had engaged in torture and other gross violations. In December 1976, an amendment to the Foreign Assistance Act known as Section 660 banned aid to police and law enforcement personnel.[412] Yet since 1980, U.S. support for El Salvador's police has grown in tandem with increasing U.S. involvement in that country. Making use of a variety of other training options and loopholes in existing legislation, the Reagan Administration steadily stepped up U.S. training, in some cases violating the spirit of the ban, if not the letter. Today, at least seven programs are educating and supplying Salvadoran security forces at home and abroad.

---

[411]See "Police Aid to Central America," p.7.

[412]Section 660. Prohibiting Police Training. (a) On and after July 1, 1975, none of the funds made available to carry out this Act, and none of the local currencies generated under this Act, shall be used to provide training or advice, or provide any financial support, for police, prisons, or other law enforcement forces for any foreign government or any program of internal intelligence or surveillance on behalf of any foreign government within the United States or abroad.

[Section 660 applies only to government funds or local currencies generated under the Foreign Assistance Act. U.S. assistance to foreign police agencies may be provided, however, under separate legislative authority.

For a thorough discussion of the subject, see "United States Assistance to Foreign Police Forces: An Analysis of Section 660," prepared by the Lawyers Committee for Human Rights - (to be published).]

Military Assistance Program and International Military Education and Training

These two programs, clearly earmarked for foreign militaries, have trained over 3,000 members of special police forces in El Salvador. The U.S. Department of Defense paved the way for the program by ruling that these men did infantry duty or counterinsurgency, not traditional police functions. This ruling was immediately challenged by some members of Congress, but attempts to close up the loophole stalled in the Senate.

Six National Police infantry battalions, known as BIPs, totalling some 2,800 troops have been trained by the Department of Defense since 1982.[413] One battalion each has also been trained in the National Guard and the Treasury Police.

MAP funds were, for example, used to train a 50-man SWAT team consisting mostly of Treasury Police. A State Department official said the squad "would operate under the direct control of the Salvadoran armed forces chief of staff...is strictly urban counterterrorism -- hostage or barricade situations and the like -- is not concerned with routine law enforcement."[414]

Yet on the two occasions when the SWAT team -- known as CEAT -- has been used in public displays of force, neither was in response to urban guerrilla activity and both resulted in loss of life. In June 1985, the CEAT stormed San Salvador's social security hospital where striking members of the STISSS union were occupying the institution. The SWAT team shot and killed five of their own plainclothes detectives who had penetrated the hospital earlier. No weapons or evidence of guerrilla activity were found on the premises. And on December 19, 1987, Manuel de Jesus Araujo died under unclear circumstances during CEAT's assault on Mariona Prison.[415]

---

[413]"Police Aid to Central America," p.14.

[414]Sam Zuckerman, "U.S. Criticized for Violating Ban on Training Foreign Police," Interlink Press Service, May 21, 1985.

[415]See p.157 on deaths in detention.

U.S. Military Sales

In 1985, 115 police cars and trucks were sold to the National Police under a $1.3 million loan guaranteed by the Export-Import Bank, which is prohibited by law from funding "defense articles or services." The State Department told the Bank that the vehicles were to be used for "traffic cop" work and not urban counterinsurgency, but no such limitation was ever put in writing to the Salvadoran authorities.[416]

Later that year, the State Department also misled the Congress concerning this sale of police vehicles. In arguing for a waiver of the 10-year ban on aid to foreign police, department officials said the Salvadoran police lacked standard vehicles to get to crime scenes in a timely fashion, failing to inform members that 115 squad cars and other vehicles had already been ordered.[417]

The 660(d) Waiver

In the aftermath of the June 1985 Zona Rosa killings of nine civilians and four Marine guards attached to the U.S. Embassy, Congress granted a two year waiver to the Section 660 ban on police training for Honduras and El Salvador. The Administration argued that the Security Forces lacked basic training and equipment to adequately respond to such actions by the guerrillas in urban areas. During FY 1986 and FY 1987, military aid was reprogrammed for use with El Salvador's three Security Forces, each with its own U.S. trainer. In late 1987, the Administration requested an additional $9.1 million in aid, extending police training into FY 1988. The Congress eventually pared the package down to $7.3 million and excluded its lethal portions.

The waiver was not renewed when it ran out in October 1987, but with money in the aid pipeline, the five U.S. trainers remained in place through FY 1988 and into FY 1989, and will

---

[416]"Bankrolling Failure: United States Policy in El Salvador and the Urgent Need for Reform," Arms Control and Foreign Policy Caucus, November 1987, p.10.

[417]"Bankrolling Failure," p.11.

likely do so until next September.[418]   Asked how training could
continue without authorization, a U.S. trainer told the Lawyers
Committee: "Because we front-loaded enough money up front." He
said some 60-70 Salvadoran instructors were being trained to
continue   the program in case the waiver was not eventually
approved.

One senior U.S. trainer in San Salvador told us they have a
three-pronged mandate to assist public security forces 1) with law
and order, 2) to combat urban terrorism and 3) to support combat
forces.[419] He said that since the Security Forces are part of the
military and "offer support during military operations," the trainers
cooperate closely with the Armed Forces.

U.S. aid has purchased riot control gear such as batons,
shields and helmets; flack vests; 262 vehicles; 1,000 radios; and 1,135
pistols and shotguns.   Since 1986, some $17 million has been
reprogrammed through the 660(d) waiver, training an average of
5,500 Security Force members per year.[420]   According to the
Department of Defense, courses include Salvadoran Civil Law;
Civil/Human Rights; Military Code of Justice; Police Patrol
Procedures; Riot Control; Physical Security; Basic Military Skills;
First Aid; Land Navigation; and Vehicle Maintenance.

Currently there are approximately 13,000 members of the
police. One U.S. training advisor told the Lawyers Committee that
about 26,000 police are needed, but the forces are currently unable
to absorb more personnel or resources.

Anti-Terrorism Assistance (ATA)

In 1983, Congress appropriated $2.5 million in FY 1984
under Section 571 of the Foreign Assistance Act for training and
equipping foreign police forces for the purpose of deterring
"terrorist groups from engaging in international terrorist acts such
as bombing, kidnapping, assassination, hostage-taking and

---

[418]Lawyers Committee interview, U.S. Embassy, San Salvador,
May 27, 1988.

[419]Lawyers Committee interview, May 27, 1988.

[420]"Information Paper: Security Force Assistance to Salvadoran
Public Security Forces FY 86-87," (Department of Defense,
February 3, 1989).

hijacking." By FY 1986-87, ATA funding had almost quadrupled to $9.84 million annually.[421]

While the program was designed to combat violent acts of an *international* character, since 1985 ATA funds have nonetheless been expended to train Salvadoran police in the United States. Between 1986 and 1988, some 250 Salvadorans were trained; $275,000 was allocated for El Salvador in FY 1988 and another $275,000 is projected for FY 1989.[422] A State Department official in charge of the program said the Salvadorans were receiving "generalized police training for domestic terrorism." Asked how ATA funds could be used to train forces fighting a domestic insurgency, the official said East Bloc countries were supplying weaponry to the FMLN.

Courses have been offered in hostage negotiations, vital installation security, bomb disposal, anti-terrorist patrol techniques, and human relations, which an official involved in the training said addressed "internal dissent." State Department administrators are clearly sensitive to the political implications of the program and flatly reject any suggestions that they are overstepping their mandate. Yet one official told the Lawyers Committee: "The purpose is to stop dissent. It was the same task the U.S. police faced during the Civil Rights movement. Controlling dissent is the task."[423]

Some equipment is also provided with the training. Trainees keep bomb kits used in the course and radios are provided during a course on VIP security.[424] Instruction is done for the most part by outside contractors, such as the Dallas Police Department, the International Association of Chiefs of Police, and Northwestern University. Currently, in FY 1988 and 1989, most Salvadorans

---

[421]In a telephone interview on March 27, 1989, a government official involved with the program said they planned to request the same funding level in FY 1990 but sought a waiver to provide training in the individual countries.

[422]Lawyers Committee interview, Department of State, April 12, 1988; telephone interview, March 27, 1989.

[423]Lawyers Committee interview, Department of State, April 6, 1988.

[424]Lawyers Committee interview, Department of State, April 12, 1988

study at the Louisiana State Police Academy at Baton Rouge under instruction from the Wackenhut Corporation, a private security firm.[425]

The program drew sharp criticism in August 1986 when CBS News reported that three of the Salvadoran ATA participants were linked to death squads, allegations the network said had been confirmed by Salvadoran and U.S. intelligence officials. Following the controversy, the Phoenix Police Department and Northwestern University withdrew from the program.[426]

Salvadoran trainees are nominated by the Vice Ministry of Public Security, screened by the U.S. Embassy in San Salvador, and their names submitted to the U.S. Congress 30 days in advance to ensure that none have been implicated in death squad killings or other rights violations.

Administration of Justice

As a percentage of the total budget, the portion of Administration of Justice (AOJ) funds allocated to training and equipping security forces is sizeable and growing. Of the $20 million regional program in Latin America and the Caribbean, a $7 million ceiling has been placed on monies for the International Criminal Investigative Training Assistance Program (ICITAP). But in El Salvador, AOJ funds also train and equip the personnel at the Special Investigative Unit and the Forensic Laboratory, most of whom are drawn from the Security Forces. As such, this constitutes another form of U.S. support for El Salvador's police.

---

[425]During 1989, instruction will include hostage negotiations; document examination for customs officers; VIP security; and vital installation security, concentrating on the 15th of September Dam.

[426]*The Phoenix Gazette*, July 19, 1986; *Los Angeles Times*, August 7, 1986.

**International Criminal Investigative Training
Assistance Program (ICITAP)**

In FY 1986, the U.S. Agency for International Development
(AID) granted $1.52 million to the Department of Justice to "design,
develop, and present projects to improve and enhance the
investigative capabilities of law enforcement agencies under judicial
or prosecutorial control in Latin America and the Caribbean."[427] A
Justice Department official involved in the program said that
Congress -- remembering the negative experiences of the Office of
Public Safety -- initially gave the program only "limited scope."[428]

By FY 1988, the ICITAP budget was $6.4 million and the
program had expanded authority to offer police management
training and to develop curricula for police academies.[429] During
1988, police personnel in twelve countries participated in ICITAP
courses.[430] With a few exceptions, training is done in each country
or at designated gathering sites for the English-speaking or Spanish-
speaking region.

The standard course, known as General Criminal
Investigations, includes one week of interviewing techniques; two
weeks on preserving evidence at the crime scene; and two weeks on
managing a crime investigation. One official involved in the

---

[427]"U.S. Department of Justice, International Criminal
Investigative Training Assistance Program, FY 88 Program
Description and Budget."

[428]Lawyers Committee interview, Washington, D.C., April 5,
1988.

[429]Section 534(b)(3) of the Foreign Assistance Act of 1961 was
amended in late 1987. The section, which authorizes the
Administration of Justice Program, describes the kinds of activities
ICITAP may conduct; Section 534(e) prohibits personnel from the
Department of Defense or members of the Armed Forces from
providing the training.

[430]ICITAP courses include students from the following
countries: Guatemala, Honduras, El Salvador, Costa Rica, the
Dominican Republic, Jamaica, Barbados, Dominica, Grenada, Belize,
Uruguay, and Colombia.

program said the course is "heavy on the practical aspects, with lots of role-playing."[431]

Other courses include vehicle theft, death and rape investigation, police-community relations, kidnapping and extortion, and crime scene search/collection and preservation of evidence. In FY 1988, some 760 Central Americans were slated for ICITAP training.[432] Instruction is provided by private consultants, some of them retired FBI agents and police officers.

ICITAP in El Salvador

In FY 1988, some $700,000 was allocated for Salvadorans to participate in ICITAP courses. An Embassy official told us the students are nominated by the Vice Ministry of Public Security on the recommendation of the heads of the three Security Forces. In fact, most of the participants are actually National Police members from the Investigative branch.[433] In one course two participants each were included from the Supreme Court and the Attorney General's office.

An Assessment of Current Programs

U.S. officials in Washington and San Salvador regularly praise the behavior of Salvadoran police in crowd control situations. A U.S. police trainer said the program had been "very effective in comparison with South Korea or Panama. There's a lot of bloodshed in demonstrations there, while there's no bloodshed with riot control here."[434] An AID official challenged: "I defy anyone to get a video tape of police performance and criticize it."[435]

Over the last decade a significant amount of money has been spent in training El Salvador's Security Forces through a variety of training options. U.S. officials point to improved police behavior

---

[431]Lawyers Committee interview, April 5, 1988.

[432]During 1988, 300 trainees were expected from the English-speaking Caribbean and approximately 170 from South America.

[433]Lawyers Committee interview, U.S. Embassy, July 5, 1988.

[434]Lawyers Committee interview, U.S. Embassy, May 27,1988.

[435]Lawyers Committee interview, U.S. Embassy, May 23, 1988.

when faced with hostile demonstrators and proclaim the programs' success. While the number and severity of violations by police in the street has diminished over the last few years, it is our belief that this decrease has more to do with the overall trend toward fewer human rights violations than with U.S. training. In our view, the most significant factor in police behavior is not the level of technical training of the troops or the availability of sophisticated riot gear, but a commitment by senior officers to hold police accountable for their actions. A significant change in police behavior can be seen when commanding officers send out the message that violence against demonstrators is unacceptable and that those who violate the guidelines for conduct will be punished. That commitment to establish a code of police conduct and enforce it is not something that aid allocations for police training can buy.

Proof that training is not a permanent guarantor against abusive police behavior can be found in the fact that now, as all major human rights indicators are rising, provocative and abusive behavior by the police is also increasing. One recent example is the demonstration by university students last September 13. *The Miami Herald* wrote:

> Hours after the two provincial attacks [by the FMLN], angry riot police surrounded leftist university students and workers in a San Salvador demonstration, hurling tear-gas cannisters and firing their rifles skyward, then clubbing demonstrators and arresting 230.[436]

Police also roughed up several reporters, provoking an apology by Minister of Defense Vides Casanova.[437]

Yet given several credible accounts of provocative behavior by police, the State Department's most recent report to the Congress on El Salvador nonetheless places blame squarely on "armed

---

[436]*The Miami Herald*, September 20, 1988.

[437]All the students detained were eventually released without charges when brought before a judge. Several students experienced minor injuries. The civilian driver of a military water cannon truck was killed by gunfire.

demonstrators organized and controlled by the FMLN."[438] In general, the State Department gives the Security Forces high marks: "...the police response has been measured and professional."

While more professional behavior is commendable, it is clear that what El Salvador's Security Forces do in broad daylight, especially under the noses of the foreign press, is quite different from what they do within the walls of Treasury Police headquarters. Today, killings, disappearances, and torture are increasing at an alarming rate. U.S. training has apparently been ineffective in stopping these practices.

---

[438]"Report on the Situation in El Salvador," U.S. Department of State, December 1, 1988, p.15.

LAWYERS COMMITTEE FOR HUMAN RIGHTS

STAFF

MICHAEL POSNER
Executive Director

WILLIAM G. O'NEILL
Deputy Director

ARTHUR C. HELTON
Director, Political Asylum Project

PATRICIA ARMSTRONG
1988 Project Coordinator

JOHN A. ASSADI
Staff Attorney

RAYMOND BROWN
Office Services

MARTHA DOGGETT
Human Rights Program

MIGDALIA GLORIA
Secretary

MITCHELL HARTMAN
Volunteer Projects
Coordinator

TERRY HUTCHINSON
Records Clerk

MARIE JEANNOT
Executive Assistant

JULIE A. LYNCH
Legal Assistant

MAKAU MUTUA
Staff Attorney

MARTHA R. MOFFETT
Staff Attorney

SANDRA MORENO
Staff Attorney

MARGARET NICHOLSON
Director of Operations

ANNETTE O'DONNELL
Production Manager

VIRGINIA PETERS
Executive Assistant

PAMELA PRICE
Coordinator,
Lawyer-to-Lawyer Project

JEMERA RONE
Central America
Representative, Part-time

JAMES D. ROSS
Staff Attorney

VIRGINIA SHERRY
Director, Special Projects

WALTER WEISS
Staff Attorney

Since 1978, the Lawyers Committee has worked to protect and promote fundamental human rights around the world. The Committee has also been at the forefront of efforts to uphold the right of refugees, in flight from political persecution, to seek asylum in the United States.

The Committee has investigated human rights violations -- and broader patterns of systemic abuse -- in over 40 countries including El Salvador, Nicaragua, Haiti, Poland, the Soviet Union, South Africa, Zimbabwe, Liberia, Pakistan, the Philippines and Cambodia. The Committee's work is nonpartisan: each government -- regardless of its political orientation -- is held to the international standards affirmed in the Universal Declaration of Human Rights and codified in broadly accepted instruments of international law. The Committee works to promote the core group of rights that guarantee the integrity of the person:

* the right to be free from torture, summary execution, abduction, disappearance;

* the right to be free from arbitrary arrest, imprisonment without charge or trial, and indefinite incommunicado detention; and

* the right to due process and a fair trial before an independent judiciary.

IF YOU WOULD LIKE A COPY OF THE COMMITTEE'S 1988 ANNUAL REPORT -- WHICH DESCRIBES OUR WORK SINCE 1978 -- PLEASE WRITE TO US AT:

330 Seventh Avenue, New York, New York 10001
(212) 629-6170
FAX (212) 967-0916